Skills Assessments,

MW01593179

Table of Contents

*PLEASE NOTE: Page 52 (Spelling) includes a list of words that students should learn to spell. These are high-frequency words that are often misspelled. This list may be given to determine proficiency at the beginning of the year. A copy could be sent home for students to use as homework over an extended period of time.

Class Record Chart

Students	Reading Overall Assessment	Word Meaning	Word Meaning in Context	Words with Multiple Meanings	Antonyms	Synonyms	Word Origins	Analogies	Compound Words and Word Classification	Affixes	Facts	Sequence	Context	Main Idea	Conclusion	Inference	Realistic Fiction	Fantasy	Nonfiction	Language Arts Overall Assessment	Capitalization and Punctuation	Capitalization	Punctuation	Nouns	Verbs	Pronouns	Using Words Correctly	Sentence Parts	Sentences	Spelling	Reference Materials	Parts of a Book

© Steck-Vaughn Company

Assessments to Identify Skills and Needs 6, SV 3397-9

Class Record Chart

Students	Dictionary Skills	Charts and Graphs	Personal Narrative	How-To Paragraph	Comparison and Contrast Paragraph	Persuasive Paragraph	Descriptive Paragraph	Math Overall Assessment	Number Concepts	Addition and Subtraction of Whole Numbers	Multiplication and Division of Whole Numbers	Geometry	Measurement	Fractions	Decimals	Statistics and Probability	Pre-Algebra	Patterns	Ratio and Percent	Estimation	Problem Solving: Whole Numbers	Problem Solving: Measurement, Geometry, and Patterns	Problem Solving: Fractions, Decimals, and Percent	Problem Solving: Estimation and Pre-Algebra	Science Overall Assessment	Earth and Space Science	Life Science	Physical Science	Social Studies Overall Assessment	Reading Maps	Reading Graphs	Reading Time Lines

© Steck-Vaughn Company

Assessments to Identify Skills and Needs 6, SV 3397-9

Name _____   Date _____

Individual Student Chart

	Test	Retest
Reading Overall Assessment		
Word Meaning		
Word Meaning in Context		
Words with Multiple Meanings		
Antonyms		
Synonyms		
Word Origins		
Analogies		
Compound Words and Word Classification		
Affixes		
Facts		
Sequence		
Context		
Main Idea		
Conclusion		
Inference		
Realistic Fiction		
Fantasy		
Nonfiction		
Language Arts Overall Assessment		
Capitalization and Punctuation		
Capitalization		
Punctuation		
Nouns		
Verbs		
Pronouns		
Using Words Correctly		
Sentence Parts		
Sentences		
Spelling		
Reference Materials		
Parts of a Book		

	Test	Retest
Dictionary Skills		
Charts and Graphs		
Personal Narrative		
How-To Paragraph		
Comparison and Contrast Paragraph		
Persuasive Paragraph		
Descriptive Paragraph		
Math Overall Assessment		
Number Concepts		
Addition and Subtraction of Whole Numbers		
Multiplication and Division of Whole Numbers		
Geometry		
Measurement		
Fractions		
Decimals		
Statistics and Probability		
Pre-Algebra		
Patterns		
Ratio and Percent		
Estimation		
Problem Solving: Whole Numbers		
Problem Solving: Measurement, Geometry, and Patterns		
Problem Solving: Fractions, Decimals, and Percent		
Problem Solving: Estimation and Pre-algebra		
Science Overall Assessment		
Earth and Space Science		
Life Science		
Physical Science		
Social Studies Overall Assessment		
Reading Maps		
Reading Graphs		
Reading Time Lines		

© Steck-Vaughn Company

Assessments to Identify Skills and Needs 6, SV 3397-9

Reading Overall Assessment

Directions Darken the circle for the correct answer.

1. Which affix makes <u>furious</u> mean "full of anger"?

  Ⓐ fur   Ⓒ fury

  Ⓑ ous   Ⓓ us

2. Which word probably comes from the Latin word *deliciae*, meaning "delight"?

  Ⓐ delicate   Ⓒ delimit

  Ⓑ deliver   Ⓓ delicious

Directions Darken the circle for the *synonym* of the underlined word.

3. To develop <u>gradually</u>

  Ⓐ again and again   Ⓒ two by two

  Ⓑ bit by bit   Ⓓ in and out

4. A nearby <u>vicinity</u>

  Ⓐ theater   Ⓒ store

  Ⓑ area   Ⓓ track

Directions Darken the circle for the *antonym* of the underlined word.

5. Isabel has a very <u>pleasant</u> personality.

  Ⓐ agreeable   Ⓒ obnoxious

  Ⓑ enormous   Ⓓ sunny

6. The farmer raised an <u>abundant</u> crop of vegetables.

  Ⓐ scarce   Ⓒ varied

  Ⓑ beautiful   Ⓓ bumper

Directions Darken the circle for the answer that will complete the analogy.

7. November : Thanksgiving = March : ____

  Ⓐ St. Patrick's Day

  Ⓑ Labor Day

  Ⓒ Election Day

  Ⓓ Memorial Day

8. purple : plum = black : ____

  Ⓐ apple

  Ⓑ tree

  Ⓒ coal

  Ⓓ white

Directions Darken the circle for *Inference* if the statement is an inference.
Darken the circle for *Fact* if the statement is a fact.

Michael loved the cool, crisp, fall weather so much that he actually enjoyed raking leaves. One day he noticed that Mr. Longly's yard down the road was full of leaves. Michael knew that Mr. Longly used a wheelchair to get around. That day after school, Michael picked up his rake and headed for Mr. Longly's house.

    Fact   Inference

9.   ◯   ◯   Mr. Longly used a wheelchair.

10. ◯   ◯   Michael raked Mr. Longly's leaves for him.

Reading Overall Assessment, p. 2

Anne's preferred subjects to study had always been ones that had to do with people. She liked history and sociology, but studying about bugs, germs, or chemicals had never won her interest.

This year, the fifth and sixth grades had to develop a scientific project to present at a science fair. Anne was a high achiever, but all she ever did was complain about science. She wondered if she had the background to complete even the simplest project. Her friends were all solving impossible problems. They were showing how to make plastic, growing tomatoes in sand, building systems for electricity, and planning mazes for mice to run through.

Anne decided that her friends were much braver than she was, but she didn't want to give up. She decided to visit the science museum to see if she could get an idea. Anne was interested in improving the quality of life for people. She was impressed by an exhibit with the title, "Help Your Children Breathe More Easily." It was about the conservation of natural resources.

Anne reviewed the exhibit carefully until she had an exact idea of what she would do. She made an "Energy Detective Game" for children to play at home. Through its activities, children learned how they could save money by turning off radios and stereos. They used clues and guessed where the greatest losses occurred. Anne's project was a great success, and she won a prize for the most practical project!

Directions Darken the circle for the correct answer.

1. What did Anne prefer to study about?
   - Ⓐ insects and germs
   - Ⓑ people
   - Ⓒ chemicals
   - Ⓓ science

2. How did Anne describe her friends for taking on such impossible projects?
   - Ⓐ brave
   - Ⓑ strong
   - Ⓒ foolish
   - Ⓓ intelligent

3. Why was Anne's project described as *practical*?
   - Ⓐ It was the only project about conservation.
   - Ⓑ It was a project for children to use.
   - Ⓒ It was the only project that made sense.
   - Ⓓ It was a project that served a useful purpose.

4. What did Anne do to get an idea?
   - Ⓐ She asked her friends for ideas.
   - Ⓑ She asked her parents to help her.
   - Ⓒ She went to the science museum.
   - Ⓓ She went for a walk in the woods.

Directions Answer the question in complete sentences.

5. What could children learn from Anne's project?

   Children learned how to save money by turning off radios and stereos

Words with Multiple Meanings

Directions Darken the circle for the word that fits both sentences.

1. The nurse cleaned my ____.

I ____ the yarn into a ball.

- Ⓐ scratches
- Ⓑ wound
- Ⓒ uniform
- Ⓓ rolls

2. Why do you ____ to watching that program?

I want to buy that pretty ceramic ____.

- Ⓐ vase
- Ⓑ vote
- Ⓒ hope
- Ⓓ object

3. The championship swim ____ will be held today.

We will ____ our friends at the station at 1:00 P.M.

- Ⓐ contest
- Ⓑ meet
- Ⓒ race
- Ⓓ show

4. We are learning to ____ by two numerals.

I have to ____ the books into two equal piles.

- Ⓐ add
- Ⓑ serve
- Ⓒ divide
- Ⓓ stack

5. We are putting a new ____ walk in the garden.

The committee presented a ____ of candidates.

- Ⓐ choice
- Ⓑ rock
- Ⓒ panel
- Ⓓ slate

6. They sailed to the ____ of the river.

The ____ teller cashed my check.

- Ⓐ side
- Ⓑ current
- Ⓒ bank
- Ⓓ mouth

7. We always enjoyed traveling by ____.

It's sometimes difficult to ____ a pet.

- Ⓐ car
- Ⓑ railroad
- Ⓒ train
- Ⓓ plane

8. I plan to take a ____ in literature next year.

What ____ of action did the doctor recommend?

- Ⓐ program
- Ⓑ course
- Ⓒ direction
- Ⓓ book

9. How many ____ can you open on a computer?

Please shut the bedroom ____.

- Ⓐ games
- Ⓑ windows
- Ⓒ programs
- Ⓓ curtains

10. The dog began to ____ at the letter carrier.

That tree has a very coarse ____.

- Ⓐ trunk
- Ⓑ yelp
- Ⓒ bark
- Ⓓ growl

Antonyms

Directions Darken the circle for the word that means *the opposite* of the underlined word.

1. To <u>revise</u> work

- Ⓐ alter
- Ⓑ erase
- Ⓒ keep the same
- Ⓓ rewrite

2. A <u>dejected</u> expression

- Ⓐ happy
- Ⓑ sad
- Ⓒ dreamy
- Ⓓ sarcastic

3. A very <u>competent</u> person

- Ⓐ unskilled
- Ⓑ happy
- Ⓒ qualified
- Ⓓ foolish

4. To <u>expand</u>

- Ⓐ grow
- Ⓑ break
- Ⓒ shrink
- Ⓓ reverse

5. To <u>lack</u> something

- Ⓐ need
- Ⓑ have
- Ⓒ lose
- Ⓓ want

6. A <u>reduced</u> amount

- Ⓐ lesser
- Ⓑ increased
- Ⓒ shorter
- Ⓓ slimmer

7. Be <u>persistent</u>

- Ⓐ sporadic
- Ⓑ continuous
- Ⓒ constant
- Ⓓ unusual

8. The <u>peculiar</u> story

- Ⓐ realistic
- Ⓑ pleasant
- Ⓒ ordinary
- Ⓓ odd

9. Attend <u>frequently</u>

- Ⓐ often
- Ⓑ never
- Ⓒ sometimes
- Ⓓ weekly

10. A <u>tense</u> moment

- Ⓐ curious
- Ⓑ silly
- Ⓒ scary
- Ⓓ relaxed

Synonyms

Directions Darken the circle for the word or group of words that means *the same or almost the same* as the underlined word.

1. Antics are

Ⓐ dreams
Ⓑ relatives
Ⓒ ideas
Ⓓ actions

2. Tedious work

Ⓐ exciting
Ⓑ difficult
Ⓒ challenging
Ⓓ boring

3. To calculate

Ⓐ figure
Ⓑ add
Ⓒ wonder
Ⓓ worry

4. Very sympathetic

Ⓐ unfriendly
Ⓑ unkind
Ⓒ understanding
Ⓓ unusual

5. To occupy

Ⓐ cover
Ⓑ inhabit
Ⓒ contest
Ⓓ afford

6. A courteous person

Ⓐ smart
Ⓑ educated
Ⓒ thrifty
Ⓓ polite

7. To collapse

Ⓐ stand up
Ⓑ go out
Ⓒ fall down
Ⓓ blow up

8. Boasting is

Ⓐ bragging
Ⓑ shouting
Ⓒ laughing
Ⓓ complaining

9. Arduous work

Ⓐ boring
Ⓑ active
Ⓒ difficult
Ⓓ exciting

10. To strive

Ⓐ take long steps
Ⓑ find the way
Ⓒ try hard
Ⓓ be envious

Word Origins

Directions Darken the circle for the word whose meaning comes from the original word.

1. Which word probably comes from the Greek word *methodos*, meaning "system"?

   (A) metal
   (B) menthol
   (C) method
   (D) meter

2. Which word probably comes from the Scandinavian word *mjukr*, meaning "gentle"?

   (A) merry
   (B) meek
   (C) merge
   (D) musty

3. Which word probably comes from the Greek word *abussos*, meaning "bottomless"?

   (A) abut
   (B) abyss
   (C) obey
   (D) abuse

4. Which word probably comes from the Spanish word *batata*, meaning "a kind of vegetable"?

   (A) carrot
   (B) bean
   (C) potato
   (D) banana

5. Which word probably comes from the French word *couper*, meaning "to cut"?

   (A) court
   (B) couple
   (C) coupe
   (D) coupon

6. Which word probably comes from the Old English word *gaman*, meaning "amusement"?

   (A) game
   (B) gamut
   (C) gambit
   (D) gambrel

7. Which word probably comes from the Latin word *moneta*, meaning "mint"?

   (A) monitor
   (B) mind
   (C) money
   (D) minus

8. Which word probably comes from the Italian word *all'erta*, meaning "on the watch"?

   (A) ally
   (B) allow
   (C) alter
   (D) alert

9. Which word probably comes from the Greek word *trein*, meaning "to be afraid"?

   (A) terrier
   (B) terror
   (C) terrain
   (D) terrace

10. Which word probably comes from the Old English word *porche*, meaning "a gate" or "entrance"?

   (A) porter
   (B) porgy
   (C) porch
   (D) pored

Analogies

Name _____ **Date** _____

(Directions) Darken the circle of the word that completes the analogy.

1. bread : head = meat : ____
- Ⓐ feat
- Ⓑ chop
- Ⓒ milk
- Ⓓ cheese

2. violin : orchestra = checker : ____
- Ⓐ band
- Ⓑ game
- Ⓒ token
- Ⓓ red

3. blades : ice skates = wheels : ____
- Ⓐ surfboards
- Ⓑ roller skates
- Ⓒ knives
- Ⓓ scissors

4. pool : swim = library : ____
- Ⓐ paper
- Ⓑ read
- Ⓒ building
- Ⓓ splash

5. lamp : light = furnace : ____
- Ⓐ heat
- Ⓑ dark
- Ⓒ cold
- Ⓓ house

6. clear : clever = class : ____
- Ⓐ clap
- Ⓑ dull
- Ⓒ room
- Ⓓ camp

7. movie : film = book : ____
- Ⓐ camera
- Ⓑ chapter
- Ⓒ paper
- Ⓓ shelf

8. broad : width = tall : ____
- Ⓐ long
- Ⓑ short
- Ⓒ height
- Ⓓ weight

9. football : field = basketball : ____
- Ⓐ diamond
- Ⓑ court
- Ⓒ table
- Ⓓ goal

10. last : lose = first : ____
- Ⓐ run
- Ⓑ play
- Ⓒ relay
- Ⓓ win

Assessments to Identify Skills and Needs 6, SV 3397-9

Compound Words and Word Classification

Directions

Darken the circle for the compound word that matches the definition.

1. Not completely cooked.
   - Ⓐ half-baked
   - Ⓑ unbaked
   - Ⓒ half time
   - Ⓓ sunbaked

2. A signal used to control traffic.
   - Ⓐ stopwatch
   - Ⓑ flashlight
   - Ⓒ stoplight
   - Ⓓ stop street

3. Letters carried by plane.
   - Ⓐ airplane
   - Ⓑ airmail
   - Ⓒ air time
   - Ⓓ air space

4. A special building for children.
   - Ⓐ playground
   - Ⓑ play-off
   - Ⓒ playhouse
   - Ⓓ play land

5. Your relationship to your father's grandfather.
   - Ⓐ grandson
   - Ⓑ great-grandchild
   - Ⓒ grandchild
   - Ⓓ granddaughter

Directions

Darken the circle for the word that best fits with the other words in the group.

6. pleased, happy, angry, furious
   - Ⓐ delighted
   - Ⓑ hungry
   - Ⓒ lazy
   - Ⓓ neat

7. squirrel, rabbit, kangaroo, wildcat
   - Ⓐ farm
   - Ⓑ woods
   - Ⓒ buffalo
   - Ⓓ barn

8. beech, oak, elm, birch
   - Ⓐ fruit
   - Ⓑ vegetable
   - Ⓒ sycamore
   - Ⓓ friend

9. football, wrestling, swimming, baseball
   - Ⓐ karate
   - Ⓑ sewing
   - Ⓒ cooking
   - Ⓓ stadium

10. opera, play, program, drama
    - Ⓐ magician
    - Ⓑ concert
    - Ⓒ team
    - Ⓓ class

Affixes

Directions Darken the circle for the correct answer to the question.

1. Which affix makes <u>multimillion</u> mean "many millions"?

   Ⓐ million
   Ⓑ multi
   Ⓒ mill
   Ⓓ lion

2. Which affix makes <u>astrology</u> mean "the study of stars"?

   Ⓐ ology
   Ⓑ astro
   Ⓒ astrol
   Ⓓ ast

3. Which affix added to <u>state</u> makes a word that means "between states"?

   Ⓐ bi
   Ⓑ dis
   Ⓒ ful
   Ⓓ inter

4. Which affix makes <u>recognize</u> mean "to know again"?

   Ⓐ re
   Ⓑ ize
   Ⓒ recon
   Ⓓ cog

5. Which affix makes <u>invaluable</u> mean "priceless"?

   Ⓐ value
   Ⓑ able
   Ⓒ valuable
   Ⓓ in

6. Which affix makes <u>autobiography</u> mean "the story of a person's life written by that person"?

   Ⓐ graph
   Ⓑ bio
   Ⓒ auto
   Ⓓ graphy

7. Which affix added to <u>spell</u> makes a word that means "badly spelled"?

   Ⓐ bi
   Ⓑ mis
   Ⓒ un
   Ⓓ ed

8. Which affix makes <u>collection</u> mean "a group of things"?

   Ⓐ collect
   Ⓑ lect
   Ⓒ tion
   Ⓓ col

9. Which affix makes <u>combustible</u> mean "apt to catch fire"?

   Ⓐ com
   Ⓑ ible
   Ⓒ le
   Ⓓ bust

10. Which affix makes <u>misleading</u> mean "deceptive"?

   Ⓐ mis
   Ⓑ lead
   Ⓒ leading
   Ⓓ ing

Facts

Directions Read the story. Darken the circle for the answer that best completes the sentence.

At age 18 Mildred Ella Didrikson was already on her way to becoming the greatest woman athlete in history. She loved to play baseball. She was nicknamed "Babe" after Babe Ruth, the famous baseball player. She grew up in Beaumont, Texas. In high school Babe was the star of the basketball team. She was also the All-City Champion high diver. She played baseball, football, pool, and tennis. She boxed and swam. In track and field, she won contest after contest. Then she moved to Dallas. There she became the All-American Girls Basketball Champion.

There was only one place left for her to test her skills. At the 1932 Olympic games, the crowd watched in excitement as Babe set new world records. She threw the javelin more than 143 feet. She ran the women's 80-meter hurdles in under 12 seconds. Babe proudly accepted two gold medals.

1. Babe threw the javelin more than _____.

Ⓐ 12 seconds
Ⓑ 80 meters
Ⓒ 180 feet
Ⓓ 143 feet

2. At the 1932 Olympics, Babe _____.

Ⓐ hurt her arm
Ⓑ played baseball
Ⓒ won two gold medals
Ⓓ worked in the field

3. Mildred Ella Didrikson was _____.

Ⓐ from Canada Ⓒ a great athlete
Ⓑ a movie star Ⓓ a famous writer

4. Mildred Ella's nickname, "Babe," comes from _____.

Ⓐ a baseball star Ⓒ her friend Sue Ellen
Ⓑ a book she read Ⓓ a basketball champion

5. Babe was the best high diver in _____.

Ⓐ track
Ⓑ Beaumont
Ⓒ the Olympics
Ⓓ Dallas

Sequence

Benjamin Banneker was born in 1731 near Baltimore. He became the best-known African American of his time. When Benjamin started school, he loved it, especially math and science. But his father needed more help around the farm. One day he told Benjamin that he would have to quit school.

Benjamin wanted to continue learning. He decided that he would study on his own. He borrowed books and stayed up late every night reading and doing math problems.

When Benjamin was 22, a merchant loaned him a pocket watch. Benjamin was fascinated! He had heard of clocks but had never seen one. He took the back off and made sketches of the gears. Benjamin decided that he would make his own clock. Carefully he carved the gears out of wood. He studied his sketches and made each part exactly right. The clock kept perfect time for 45 years!

Next Benjamin became interested in the night sky. He noticed that the stars moved. Was there a pattern to this movement? He decided to find out. Each night he sat outside and observed the sky. He made sketches and charts and taught himself astronomy.

The more Benjamin learned, the more he wanted to learn. In 1783, when he was 52, he sold the family farm. Now at last he was able to devote all his time to learning. He taught himself the skill of surveying. In 1791 he helped survey the nation's new capital city, Washington, D.C. That same year he began publishing an almanac. This book predicted the weather and told about the tides. Benjamin printed the almanac for ten years. In spite of his difficult circumstances, Benjamin had followed his dreams. His talent and self discipline had made it possible for him to accomplish his many goals.

Go on to next page.

Name _____ Date _____

Sequence, p. 2

Directions Answer each question about the story. Darken the circle for the correct answer.

1. When did Benjamin teach himself astronomy?
   - Ⓐ before he made the clock
   - Ⓑ while he was in school
   - Ⓒ before he sold the family farm

2. When did Benjamin first publish his almanac?
   - Ⓐ before he made the clock
   - Ⓑ in 1791
   - Ⓒ when he was 22

3. When did Benjamin first see a watch?
   - Ⓐ after he wrote the almanac
   - Ⓑ when he was 22
   - Ⓒ when he first went to school

4. When did Benjamin sell the family farm?
   - Ⓐ before he quit school
   - Ⓑ before he made the watch
   - Ⓒ before he learned surveying

Directions Put these events in the order that they happened.

5. Write the number **1** on the line by the sentence that tells what happened first. Then write the number **2** by the sentence that tells what happened next. Write the number **3** by the sentence that tells what happened last.

_____ Benjamin sold the family farm.

_____ Benjamin went to school.

_____ Benjamin made a clock based on his sketches.

Context

Directions Read the paragraph. Darken the circle for the answer that best completes the sentence.

1. Every June **mobs** of people gather at Jensen Beach in Florida to watch for sea turtles. Hundreds of people snap pictures of the turtles as they lay their eggs.

   In this paragraph the word **mobs** means

   Ⓐ crowds   Ⓒ swimmers
   Ⓑ visitors   Ⓓ couples

2. Have you ever seen a moonbow? It's like a rainbow, but it's made by the moon. Moonbows **occur** when the moon's light shines through the mist from a waterfall.

   In this paragraph the word **occur** means

   Ⓐ rain   Ⓒ happen
   Ⓑ flow   Ⓓ disappear

3. Once a man checked out a book from a library. He **neglected** to return it. The book was finally returned by his great-grandson 145 years later. Although the fine came to $2,264, the great-grandson did not have to pay it.

   In this paragraph the word **neglected** means

   Ⓐ hurried   Ⓒ borrowed
   Ⓑ failed   Ⓓ remembered

4. The oldest false teeth are almost three thousand years old. They were found on the body of a **deceased** person in an old grave. The teeth were strung together with gold wire.

   In this paragraph the word **deceased** means

   Ⓐ dead   Ⓒ healthy
   Ⓑ old   Ⓓ rich

5. Sir Robert Peel formed a special police force in London to fight crime. It was so **effective** that other towns started special forces, too. These police officers are now called bobbies, for Sir Robert's nickname.

   In this paragraph the word **effective** means

   Ⓐ ragged   Ⓒ quiet
   Ⓑ successful   Ⓓ proud

Main Idea

Directions Darken the circle for the answer that best completes the sentence.

1. Winston Churchill, the Prime Minister of Great Britain, is remembered for his great speeches. But as a boy, Churchill had trouble speaking. He stuttered. As a teenager, he found a way to control his stuttering. He began each sentence by saying "mmmmm." Although this took care of his problem, he continued to do this for the rest of his life.

   The story mainly tells that
   A Churchill had a speech problem
   B Churchill would not speak in public
   C Churchill stuttered because he had no tongue
   D Churchill started stuttering as a teenager

2. The heads of four men are carved into Mount Rushmore. They are Presidents Washington, Jefferson, Lincoln, and Roosevelt. Most of the work was done with dynamite. Workers carved the details with air hammers. They worked from cages and swings that hung from the top of the mountain. It took six and one-half years to finish the job.

   The story mainly tells
   A how the carvings were made
   B which Presidents are carved on the mountain
   C how to work on top of Mount Rushmore
   D how mountain carvers do their jobs

3. Did you know that when a sheep falls down, it cannot get up again by itself? A sheep has a heavy body but delicate legs. When it's lying on its back, it's weighted down by its thick, heavy fleece. Even waving its legs doesn't help. Its legs are too thin and weak to swing its heavy body onto its side. A shepherd has to help the sheep back onto its feet!

   The story mainly tells
   A how a sheep uses its legs to get up
   B that a sheep never falls down
   C why a sheep can't get itself up when it falls down
   D how a sheep uses its fleece to get up

4. When Millard Fillmore was 19, he could hardly read or write. He lived on a farm. He spent more time working than going to school. But later he decided to return to school. Abigail Powers was Fillmore's teacher. They fell in love, and later they were married. Fillmore went on to become a teacher, a lawyer, and the President of the United States!

   The story mainly tells that
   A Fillmore never learned to read and write
   B Fillmore went to school as an adult
   C Fillmore taught Abigail Powers to read
   D Fillmore never married

Conclusion

Directions Darken the circle for the answer that best completes the sentence.

1. Why do people sneeze? Scientists aren't sure why, but they know that sneezing can be a sign of illness. The Greeks at one time believed that one of their gods had invented sneezing. The early Romans believed that sneezing helped people make smart decisions. People in Europe thought that sneezing was a symbol of good health. So any patient who sneezed three times was always released from the hospital.

    From this story you can tell that

    (A) sneezing has improved through the years
    (B) the early Greeks were the first to sneeze
    (C) ideas about sneezing have changed over time
    (D) most people sneeze only three times

2. Fannie Lou Hamer grew up in the South. Like many other African Americans there, she was poor. Life was hard, and her people had few rights. In 1962 Fannie was fed up. She wanted to change things. She registered to vote but was arrested for no reason. Bullets were fired at her. She was even beaten. Still she worked to gain voting rights for all people. In 1965 her dream came true. Congress passed a voting-rights bill.

    The story suggests that Fannie Lou Hamer

    (A) liked being poor
    (B) was arrested for running a stop sign
    (C) never achieved her goal
    (D) had a dangerous fight to win her rights

3. Modern weddings are full of traditions. Some of these traditions date back to ancient times. Even today many brides wear veils when they marry. This comes from an ancient Spartan practice. At that time the bride used the veil to hide from evil spirits. Even the bridesmaids were meant to hide the bride away from evil spirits. The bride would surround herself with girls her own age in order to confuse the evil spirits. Only the groom could recognize her then.

    You can conclude that

    (A) the groom is an evil spirit
    (B) the Spartans were afraid of evil spirits
    (C) evil spirits like wedding cakes
    (D) bridesmaids help evil spirits find the bride

Inference

Directions Darken the circle for *Fact* if the statement is a fact. Darken the circle for *Inference* if the statement is an inference.

1. Wilt Chamberlain holds the record for scoring the most points in one professional basketball game. In 1962 the Philadelphia Warrior scored 100 points against the New York Knicks. Chamberlain's record was 29 points higher than the record of the next-highest scorer.

Fact   Inference

○   ○   **A.** Chamberlain played professional basketball.
○   ○   **B.** Chamberlain scored 100 points in one game.
○   ○   **C.** Chamberlain was a very good player.
○   ○   **D.** Chamberlain's record will be hard to beat.

2. James and Jenny wanted to give their mom a special birthday present. "I have an idea," James said. "We could clean the whole house from top to bottom." "You're right! Mom would never believe it!" Jenny said. The next Saturday they asked their dad to take their mom out all afternoon. They vacuumed, dusted, and washed floors and windows until the whole house sparkled.

Fact   Inference

○   ○   **A.** James and Jenny cleaned the house.
○   ○   **B.** Their mom was surprised.
○   ○   **C.** James and Jenny love their mom.
○   ○   **D.** They were tired after working all afternoon.

3. Daniel Defoe wrote the book *Robinson Crusoe*. He got his ideas from the real-life adventures of a man named Alexander Selkirk. Selkirk was a sailor on a ship off the coast of Chile. In 1704 he argued with his captain and demanded to be left on shore. The captain allowed Selkirk to stay. Selkirk lived by eating turtles, fish, and goats. He was finally rescued in 1709.

Fact   Inference

○   ○   **A.** Selkirk was a stubborn man.
○   ○   **B.** The captain allowed Selkirk to stay.
○   ○   **C.** Daniel Defoe wrote *Robinson Crusoe*.
○   ○   **D.** Selkirk became good at hunting and fishing.

Tran's Secret

Tran could not believe that he was about to waste an evening. A group of his friends wanted him to join them for ghost stories around a campfire. At first, Tran had refused, saying, "Oh, that's stupid. Who wants to sit around listening to a bunch of stories that you know are made up just to scare everyone? That stuff's for little kids!" Nevertheless, his friends had prevailed upon him to go. "Come on, Tran," they said. "It'll be fun."

So here he was, walking down this stupid path in these stupid woods so he could sit next to some stupid fire and listen to some stupid ghost stories! He glanced uneasily around him at the dark forms of the trees and listened to the croaking of the frogs. "Nothing scary in these woods," he said to himself. He took his place around the fire that had been built on the sand near the lake. Lisa began a story of a castle in England that had been haunted for years by the ghost of a woman. In a soft voice meant to be spooky, Tran thought, Lisa related the tale. It was said that the woman had died of a broken heart. A man had been chosen for her to marry, but she had fallen in love with another man from the village. Her father did not approve, so he had had some of his hired hands kill the man from the village. When the girl found out, she had shut herself in one of the turrets of the castle and refused to eat or drink until she just wasted away.

A loon called out across the lake and sent shivers up Tran's spine. "Dumb bird," thought Tran. "I wish this story would end so we could get out of here."

"To this day," Lisa continued, "both the soft crying of the woman and the anguished wailing of her father can be heard in the castle. For when he found that his daughter was dead, the father was never the same again. He wandered around the castle and eventually went mad. One more thing—the door to the room that the girl died in cannot be opened easily. It has to be forced…and there is NOTHING to explain why." Just then, an owl hooted in a nearby tree, and Tran jumped up and screamed, causing everyone else to yell, too.

"Hey, Tran!" laughed Lisa. "I didn't scare you or anything, did I?"

"Me? Scared?" asked Tran. He looked around at the smiling faces of his friends. He was the only one standing, and he realized he was clutching his backpack tightly to his chest. So much for his big brave talk—now everyone knew he could be scared by a silly ghost story! He guessed the joke was on him. Slowly, he smiled. "Yeah, I guess I am scared!" he admitted. "Good story, Lisa."

Go on to next page.

Tran's Secret, p. 2

Directions Answer each question about the story. Darken the circle for the correct answer.

1. In Lisa's story, who haunted the castle?

- (A) a girl
- (B) a man
- (C) a girl and her father
- (D) a girl and the man she loved

2. Tran's friends wanted him to ____.

- (A) go camping with them
- (B) listen to ghost stories
- (C) swim in the lake
- (D) build a campfire

3. Tran said he did not want to go because ____.

- (A) it was for little kids
- (B) it was too cold out
- (C) he had something else to do
- (D) he was afraid of the dark

4. Tran said the loon was a "dumb bird" because ____.

- (A) it was not intelligent
- (B) it could not swim
- (C) it flew near the fire
- (D) it scared him

5. Tran had talked as if he could not be scared because ____.

- (A) he did not want his friends to laugh at him
- (B) he was not afraid of anything
- (C) he did not know how to tell ghost stories
- (D) he loved being in the dark woods

Another Person's Shoes

You will experience, many times in your life, lessons that teach you not to judge a person's actions or a situation until you have all the facts. Judging things just from appearances can cause embarrassment. It can be unfair to the person who is judged. There are many old sayings that suggest that we should not rush our judgments, such as "Don't judge a book by its cover," and "Don't judge a person until you have walked a mile in his or her shoes." A person might say, "Well, what would *you* do if you were in *my* shoes?" All these things mean that before you say what you would do, or what you think someone else should have done in a situation, you should consider all of the circumstances.

Often you will hear young people say that they will never do the things that their parents do. Sometimes this turns out to be true, but another very common comment by people who become parents is that they have found themselves doing just those things that they said they would not do when they were younger. Why have they changed? It is because as young people with no children, they could not understand what makes parents act the way they do. Once a person becomes a parent, it often becomes clear what caused their own parents to make the decisions that they made. The new parents are actually "walking in the shoes" of their own parents. Now they understand!

Before you judge another person or say what you would *never* do, put yourself in the other person's position. Think of all the factors. It may be that we can never fully understand another person's motives, but we can try. So many things affect a person's decision that the decision made one day may not even be the same one that would be made the next day or the next week. Financial pressures, social pressures, stress at home or at work, and even the weather can be factors in decision-making. This is not to say that there is always an excuse for a bad decision, just that all decisions that *seem* bad may not *be* bad. They may have been the best choice available at the time.

The next time you question someone's actions, think whatever you like. But before you pass judgment aloud, be sure you have thought long enough about what is fair.

Go on to next page.

Another Person's Shoes, p. 2

Directions Answer each question about the story. Use complete sentences.

1. What is the author's purpose in this story?

_____

_____

_____

2. What does the author say is important to consider?

_____

_____

_____

3. Name one of the old sayings about not rushing to judgment.

_____

_____

_____

4. Name two factors in decision-making that the author mentions.

_____

_____

_____

5. What does the word *financial* refer to?

_____

_____

_____

Alyson's Wish

Uncle Will bought the necklace from an old woman, who said that it had magic power. She refused to tell how to use the power. "It's a bad thing," she said.

Alyson held her gift from Uncle Will to the light. Its stone cast an orange beam into the room. "If I believe that, I can rub the stone and make a wish that will come true." She wished for sunshine, but didn't get it.

Alyson had an idea. She would tell her little sister, Clara, that this was a magic necklace. Clara would believe her. Then two would believe—three, if she counted the old lady; then the magic would work.

Clara asked what Alyson was wishing for as her big sister rubbed the stone before they got in bed. "I wish every week had only Saturdays," Alyson said.

When they go up the next morning, it was Saturday. "But it was Sunday yesterday," Clara said.

"I know," Alyson said, jumping with glee.

Weeks later, Alyson sat on her bed one morning. "It's Saturday again," she said, yawning. "I'm so tired of Saturdays. I wish I could go to school." She began rubbing the stone and wishing for Monday.

Clara awakened and heard her. "It's no use," Clara said. "I knew from the beginning that it only gives one wish to each person." The girls looked at each other and smiled. Slowly Alyson handed Clara the necklace so that Clara could make her wish.

Soon their mother was at the door. "Time to get ready for school, girls," she said.

"I will never give this necklace to anyone else," Alyson said. "People are too careless with wishes."

Go on to next page.

Alyson's Wish, p. 2

Directions Answer each question about the story. Darken the letter for the correct answer.

1. Clara realizes that the necklace would ____.

    Ⓐ never grant her a wish
    Ⓑ change colors when it was rubbed
    Ⓒ only give one wish to each person
    Ⓓ only work for a short while

2. When Clara's wish comes true, she probably feels ____.

    Ⓐ surprised and angry
    Ⓑ upset and fearful
    Ⓒ happy but anxious
    Ⓓ relieved and satisfied

3. Alyson wishes for ____.

    Ⓐ another necklace
    Ⓑ a gift from Uncle Will
    Ⓒ weeks made up of Saturdays
    Ⓓ a chance to talk to the old woman

4. Soon after Alyson gets her wish, she feels that ____.

    Ⓐ she should begin wishing for other things
    Ⓑ a life of Saturdays is wonderful
    Ⓒ the necklace's power is not a bad thing
    Ⓓ having nothing but Saturdays is boring

5. Alyson believes that the necklace will work if ____.

    Ⓐ enough people believe it will
    Ⓑ she gets Clara to make the wishes
    Ⓒ she finds the right spot to rub
    Ⓓ she gets the light to shine through it

Queen of the Courts, p. 3

Directions Answer each question about the story. Use complete sentences.

1. Where did Althea grow up?

_____

_____

2. What games did Althea play as a child?

_____

_____

3. Who came up with a plan to help Althea?

_____

_____

_____

4. What was important about Althea playing tennis at Forest Hills?

_____

_____

_____

5. What happened to Althea at the 1957 Wimbledon championship?

_____

_____

Flames in the Sky!

"Here it comes, ladies and gentlemen. And what a sight it is, a thrilling one, a marvelous sight."

So began Herbert Morrison, an announcer for radio station WLS. He was calmly describing the airship *Hindenburg*. It was just about to land at Lakehurst, New Jersey, on May 6, 1937. Morrison was one of the reporters there to cover the story.

Suddenly, Morrison's voice filled with fright. "It's burst into flames! It is burning, bursting into flames and is falling! Oh! It's a terrible sight! The flames are 500 feet into the sky!"

On May 3, 1937, the *Hindenburg* left Frankfurt, Germany. It carried 38 passengers and a crew of 59. The giant airship had already made ten trips across the Atlantic Ocean to the United States. This looked like another ordinary trip.

At first, the flight went smoothly, but as the *Hindenburg* neared Lakehurst, the weather turned bad. Black clouds gathered, thunder rumbled, and the wind began picking up. Captain Max Pruss didn't want to risk a landing. He would stay where he was and wait for better weather.

At last a message came from Lakehurst that all was clear and waiting. The *Hindenburg* headed for Lakehurst. It seemed that the three-day trip was safely over. Passengers gathered their belongings and checked their passports. Some looked out the windows where family and friends waved from the ground. Everyone was smiling.

At 7:21 P.M., landing ropes were lowered from the airship. Captain Pruss sent a message reading, "The *Hindenburg* has just made a safe landing." Nothing could have been farther from the truth.

Until 7:25 P.M., May 6, 1937, no one doubted the *Hindenburg's* safety. The builders of the airship were proud that not one of their airships had crashed. The *Hindenburg* was the safest yet. The huge blimp measured 146 feet high and 803 feet long. People looked up in wonder whenever it passed overhead. They believed that one day thousands of people would travel by airship.

The *Hindenburg* had only one weakness. It was filled with hydrogen, a gas that exploded easily, and one spark could cause a terrible explosion. To make sure there were no sparks, no passenger could carry matches or lighters, and there was a special room for smoking, which was sealed with two locked doors. Passengers wore sneakers or felt boots to prevent sparks. Crew members who worked near the gas cells wore no buttons or metal because of the danger of sparks.

The *Hindenburg* was ready to land. It hovered quietly in the air about 75 feet above the ground. At 7:25 P.M., W. W. Groves, an engineer on the ground, noticed a small spark dancing near the stern. "It looked like static electricity," he later said.

Go on to next page.

Flames in the Sky!, p. 2

Suddenly, a huge flame burst from the top of the airship. One of the gas cells in the tail exploded, and within seconds, another cell did the same. People on the ground ran for their lives.

"The whole tail section burst into flames," Groves remembered. "I began to run. It was exploding above my head. Burning fabric began to fall."

Meanwhile, in the control car, Captain Pruss felt the airship jerk, but wasn't sure what it was. Then, he heard a loud bang and people screaming on the field below.

"What is it?" he asked, looking out the window.

"The ship's burning!" cried the radio officer.

On the ground, Herbert Morrison, the radio announcer, couldn't believe his eyes. "This is the worst thing I've ever witnessed," he said.

It looked like no one could live through the fire, but somehow 62 people did. It took 34 seconds for the burning wreck to crash to the ground. This gave some people time to jump to safety. Passenger Philip Mangone tried to open a window, but it was stuck, so he took a chair and broke the glass. Then, he jumped 35 feet to the ground. The fire burned his face and hands, but he had no other injuries.

Werner Franz, a 14-year-old cabin boy, made the most unlikely escape. The fire was all around him. Franz thought he was finished. Just then, the heat caused a water tank to burst over his head, and it soaked him. He managed to escape without being badly burned.

In all, 36 people died, including 22 crew members, 13 passengers, and one member of the ground crew.

What caused the crash? It may have been static electricity or lightning. Some people even think that the fire was set on purpose. No one knows for sure.

Today, airships use helium. Helium does not explode as easily as hydrogen. One thing, however, is certain. Because of the crash of the *Hindenburg*, airships were never again used for passenger travel.

Go on to next page.

Flames in the Sky, p. 3

Directions Answer each question about the story. Darken the circle for the correct answer.

1. The *Hindenburg* was ____ airship.

Ⓐ an English
Ⓑ a German
Ⓒ an American

2. The *Hindenburg* was filled with ____.

Ⓐ helium
Ⓑ oxygen
Ⓒ hydrogen

3. The *Hindenburg* burst into flames while landing in ____.

Ⓐ New Jersey
Ⓑ New York
Ⓒ Washington D.C.

4. ____ might have started the fire.

Ⓐ Static electricity
Ⓑ Water
Ⓒ Helium

5. The *Hindenberg* had a crew of ____.

Ⓐ 30
Ⓑ 15
Ⓒ 59

6. The *Hindenberg* had made ____ trips before it was destroyed.

Ⓐ 10
Ⓑ 20
Ⓒ 15

7. ____ was the radio announcer who described the incident.

Ⓐ Pruss
Ⓑ Morrison
Ⓒ Franz

Name _____ Date _____

First on the Moon

Streets were empty. Telephones were silent. Stores were deserted. All across America, people had stopped their normal activities. Millions sat in front of their television sets, waiting for the big moment. No one wanted to miss the take-off of *Apollo 11*.

At the Cape Kennedy Space Center in Florida, everything was ready. The *Apollo 11* spaceship was ready to go. Inside it, three astronauts lay strapped to their seats. These astronauts were Neil Armstrong, Edwin Aldrin, Jr., and Michael Collins. These three men were going to go on an incredible journey. They were going to fly to the Moon.

Apollo 11 left the Earth at 9:32 A.M. on July 16, 1969. If all went well, it would be circling the Moon in four days.

The most amazing part of the plan came next. Armstrong and Aldrin planned to leave the main spacecraft, enter a smaller spacecraft called the *Eagle*, and take the *Eagle* down to the surface of the Moon. After a short stay, they would return to the main ship.

The astronauts knew the mission was dangerous like all trips into space. They didn't waste time thinking about it. Instead, they kept telling themselves that the trip would be a success. They trusted the people who built the spaceship and the people who planned the flight path. Most of all, they trusted each other.

The first two hours in space went smoothly. *Apollo 11* raced toward the Moon at 24,000 miles per hour. But then, suddenly, the astronauts lost radio contact with Earth. For a few heart-stopping moments, the control room was silent. Luckily, the astronauts managed to adjust the instruments. Once again, they made contact with Earth.

As *Apollo 11* traveled farther into space, it slowed down. After 57 hours, it was moving only about 2,000 miles per hour. Then, as it began to circle the moon, *Apollo 11* sped up to 5,000 miles per hour.

Inside the spaceship, Armstrong and Aldrin prepared for their historic journey. They left the main ship and crawled into the *Eagle*. Collins would be in charge of *Apollo 11* while they were gone.

As he watched his two friends leave, he remembered a question one reporter had asked him before the mission began. "What if Armstrong and Aldrin run into trouble?"

Collins had answered in a quiet voice. "If they have trouble on the surface of the Moon, there is nothing I can do about it. I don't think that will happen. If it did, I would do everything I could to help them. But they know and I know that there are certain problems where I just simply light the motor and come home without them."

Now these words rang in Collins's head. So many things could go wrong. What if Armstrong and Aldrin could not find a flat place to land? What if the *Eagle* was damaged during landing? What if its one engine failed?

Go on to next page.

First on the Moon, p. 2

At 2:02 A.M. on July 20, Armstrong pushed a lever in the *Eagle*. Slowly, the craft moved away from the main ship and headed down toward the Moon. Armstrong spoke into his radio. "The *Eagle* has wings," he said.

A computer helped guide the spacecraft. Armstrong helped to keep the *Eagle* moving at the right speed and height. As it neared the Moon, Armstrong saw more and more craters. The *Eagle* was flying over a huge field of rocks. Armstrong began to wonder if he could make a safe landing. The Eagle didn't have much fuel left. If it didn't land soon, he would have to turn it around and head back to *Apollo 11*. At last, he saw a patch of ground that looked flat. He steered the *Eagle* over to it. As the *Eagle* came down, its engine stirred up moondust. Somehow, through the dust, Armstrong managed to set the spacecraft down safely. At 4:17 P.M., he spoke into his radio. "The *Eagle* has landed," he said.

After landing, Armstrong put on a special suit and an air tank and opened the *Eagle's* hatch. Back home on Earth, millions of people watched on TV as Armstrong took his first step on the Moon. "That's one small step for a man, one giant leap for mankind," he said.

Next, Aldrin came down the ladder. The two men walked along the Moon's surface. They planted an American flag in the ground. Near it they put a sign that read, "HERE MEN FROM THE PLANET EARTH FIRST SET FOOT UPON THE MOON. JULY 1969, A.D. WE CAME IN PEACE FOR ALL MANKIND." Armstrong and Aldrin also collected rocks to take home with them. Then, they returned to the Eagle.

By this time, both men were very happy. They smiled to think their footprints would stay on the Moon's surface for years. But the danger was not over yet. They still had to get back to the main spaceship. At 1:55 P.M. on July 21, they got ready to start the *Eagle's* engine. If it didn't work, they would be trapped on the Moon forever.

Armstrong held his breath as he turned on the engine. Instantly it fired up. He counted down the seconds, "Nine, eight, seven, six, five." When the moment came for the *Eagle* to take off, everything went perfectly. "That was beautiful!" said Armstrong. "Very smooth."

The *Eagle* moved slowly away from the Moon and soon hooked up with the main spaceship. Then, *Apollo 11* turned and headed home. At 12:40 P.M. on July 24, the spaceship splashed down in the Pacific Ocean. Collins, Aldrin, and Armstrong climbed out proudly. For the first time in the history of the world, men had gone to the Moon and back.

Go on to next page.

First on the Moon, p. 3

Directions Answer each question about the story. Use complete sentences.

1. Name the astronauts who took the *Eagle* to the surface of the Moon.

_____

_____

2. What did the astronauts use during the trip to talk to Earth?

_____

_____

3. Who was in charge of *Apollo 11* when the *Eagle* went to the Moon?

_____

_____

4. What were Armstrong's words after he took his first step on the Moon?

_____

_____

_____

5. On what date did the men from *Apollo 11* walk on the Moon?

_____

_____

6. How long would the astronauts' footprints stay on the Moon's surface?

_____

_____

Language Arts Overall Assessment

Directions Darken the circle for the correct answer.

1. Which of the following words is a noun?

Next year we will start to learn Spanish.
Ⓐ   Ⓑ   Ⓒ   Ⓓ

2. Which of the following words is a pronoun?

The children washed their hands before lunch.
Ⓐ   Ⓑ   Ⓒ   Ⓓ

3. Which word is an adjective?

Valerie bought a new sweater at the mall.
    Ⓐ   Ⓑ   Ⓒ   Ⓓ

4. Which of the following words is a noun?

Each of the women baked a pie for the class picnic.
Ⓐ   Ⓑ   Ⓒ   Ⓓ

5. Which of the following words is a verb?

Maria is the tallest girl in the class.
    Ⓐ   Ⓑ   Ⓒ   Ⓓ

6. What is the complete subject of this sentence?
All my friends are going on the class trip next week.

Ⓐ the class trip   Ⓒ friends are going
Ⓑ All my friends   Ⓓ trip next week

7. What is the complete subject of this sentence?
The storm destroyed all the vegetables in our garden.

Ⓐ vegetables in our garden   Ⓒ all the vegetables
Ⓑ storm destroyed   Ⓓ The storm

8. What is the complete predicate of this sentence?
The truck driver drove down the new highway.

Ⓐ The truck driver   Ⓒ drove down the new highway
Ⓑ driver drove   Ⓓ new highway

9. What is the complete predicate of this sentence?
My new sneakers are black and white.

Ⓐ are black and white   Ⓒ My new
Ⓑ new sneakers   Ⓓ sneakers are black and white

Name _____   Date _____

Language Arts Overall Assessment, p. 2

Directions Darken the circle for the word that is spelled correctly.

1. How ____ do you visit the dentist?

   Ⓐ offen   Ⓒ oftin

   Ⓑ often   Ⓓ offin

2. Did you get your ____ slip signed?

   Ⓐ permission   Ⓒ permision

   Ⓑ permition   Ⓓ pirmission

Directions Darken the circle for the sentence that shows correct punctuation.

3. Ⓐ Tanya, did you see the show?

   Ⓑ Becky asked "How are you, Eric?"

   Ⓒ Well, how will you get there Jay?

   Ⓓ She told the truth, and was not believed.

4. Ⓐ Take control of the car.

   Ⓑ Please, will you come!

   Ⓒ Don't I know you.

   Ⓓ Let me read that first?

5. Ⓐ "How are you"? asked Dan

   Ⓑ "How, asked Sue, do you do it?"

   Ⓒ "When can you come?" I asked.

   Ⓓ "Yes! said Marie, "I can."

6. Ⓐ Wow. That's a great album.

   Ⓑ Can you go with us!

   Ⓒ Have you seen a shooting star?

   Ⓓ What a great ceremony?

Directions Write the answer for each question.

7. What is the complete title of this book?

_____

_____

8. What is the call number of this book?

_____

9. Is this card a title card, an author card, or a subject card?

_____

709.011 G	Art of the Plains Indians, The **Glubok, Shirley** The Art of the Plains Indians/Shirley Glubok; Designed by Gerald Nook; special photography by Alfred Tamarin. New York: Macmillan Publishing Company, 1975.

Directions Tell if each item is *fiction, nonfiction, biography, reference,* or *periodical.*

10. the novel <u>A Wonderful, Terrible Time</u> _____

11. a book that tells of the life of a President _____

12. an encyclopedia article about Camp David _____

13. a magazine from the American Camping Association _____

14. a book about the Civil War _____

Capitalization and Punctuation

Directions Darken the circle for the sentence that shows correct capitalization and punctuation.

1. Ⓐ Did you ever ride on the Amtrak?
   Ⓑ Eliot you must go now.
   Ⓒ Thank you for the gift lola.
   Ⓓ Carmen wants to own a kitten but she is allergic to animals.

2. Ⓐ Who won the Nobel prize last year.
   Ⓑ We are always very busy in december
   Ⓒ In which direction should we walk!
   Ⓓ Gus said, "Let's play chess."

3. Ⓐ Fifth avenue is a famous street for shopping.
   Ⓑ Her dogs tail is always wagging.
   Ⓒ Would you like to go to the zoo with us?
   Ⓓ Nov is the abbreviation for November.

4. Ⓐ Although it was getting dark i didn't panic.
   Ⓑ "Ramon, are you ready yet?"
   Ⓒ Roy was born on August 10 1989.
   Ⓓ We ordered hamburgers fries and shakes for lunch.

5. Ⓐ The flight from new york to California takes six hours.
   Ⓑ Mona will read her report on Greece and troy.
   Ⓒ Velma said, "Please hand me that book."
   Ⓓ Jamal was excited when he flew over the pacific ocean.

6. Ⓐ Is today your brothers birthday?
   Ⓑ Who is that new person in the office.
   Ⓒ Gina asked, "Where did you get your new CD?"
   Ⓓ Sylvia can speak Russian, French Spanish, and Italian.

7. Ⓐ All men women and children will enjoy this movie.
   Ⓑ July 4. 1776 is a special date in U.S. history.
   Ⓒ I think that I'd like to study Latin next year.
   Ⓓ *Grimm's Fairy tales* are still popular.

8. Ⓐ Isn't this a beautiful day
   Ⓑ Our teacher said, "You have ten minutes for this test."
   Ⓒ New Orleans Louisiana is known for its jazz concerts.
   Ⓓ Ernesto always does his homework

9. Ⓐ Close the door quietly please
   Ⓑ Where did you hide the candy.
   Ⓒ Why don't you visit us more often?
   Ⓓ Be careful

10. Ⓐ No we don't have any shirts left in your size.
    Ⓑ Lola wants to walk but Ray prefers to drive.
    Ⓒ Yes I'd love to join you at the skating rink.
    Ⓓ When you hear thunder, rain will probably follow.

Capitalization and Punctuation

Directions Darken the circle for the part of the sentence that should be capitalized.

1. Most movies   are made   in   hollywood, California.
   Ⓐ   Ⓑ   Ⓒ   Ⓓ

2. Washington, d. c.   is the   capital of   the United States.
   Ⓐ   Ⓑ   Ⓒ   Ⓓ

3. The post office   is on   stewart Avenue   in Middletown.
   Ⓐ   Ⓑ   Ⓒ   Ⓓ

4. On Election day   we vote   for the people   who make our laws.
   Ⓐ   Ⓑ   Ⓒ   Ⓓ

5. My mother   said to   the painters,   "please be careful."
   Ⓐ   Ⓑ   Ⓒ   Ⓓ

Directions Darken the circle for the punctuation mark that makes the sentence correct.

6. Mr Denton's store is on Main St. in New Bedford.
   Ⓐ ,   Ⓑ .   Ⓒ "   Ⓓ ;

7. She asked, "Why did you do that"
   Ⓐ !   Ⓑ :   Ⓒ ?   Ⓓ ;

8. That is the worst book I ever read
   Ⓐ ?   Ⓑ :   Ⓒ !   Ⓓ ,

9. *The Ugly Duckling* by Hans Christian Anderson, is my favorite fairy tale.
   Ⓐ ?   Ⓑ "   Ⓒ ,   Ⓓ ;

10. Lavinia wants to go shopping but Joan prefers to go for a walk.
    Ⓐ ,   Ⓑ ;   Ⓒ .   Ⓓ !

Capitalization

Directions Darken the circle for the word that should be capitalized.

1. Who wrote the adventure story *The Call of the wild?*

   Ⓐ wrote   Ⓑ adventure   Ⓒ story   Ⓓ wild

2. I met mayor Bradley at the celebration yesterday.

   Ⓐ met   Ⓑ mayor   Ⓒ celebration   Ⓓ yesterday

3. She lives at 503 north Bryer Street, on the corner near the store.

   Ⓐ corner   Ⓑ store   Ⓒ north   Ⓓ near

4. I had sweet and sour chicken at a chinese restaurant.

   Ⓐ sweet   Ⓑ chicken   Ⓒ chinese   Ⓓ restaurant

5. My parents celebrated their wedding anniversary in may.

   Ⓐ parents   Ⓑ wedding   Ⓒ anniversary   Ⓓ may

Directions Circle each word that should be capitalized.

6. the woman said, "my party is in one week."

7. "have some more carrot sticks," said the host.

8. The high school band played "stand by me."

9. the teenagers will go to the game together.

10. Who wrote the poem "the children's hour"?

Punctuation

Directions Darken the circle for the correct answer to the question.

In which sentence is end punctuation used correctly?

1. Ⓐ How wonderful our trip was?
   Ⓑ I can't remember.
   Ⓒ Are you going to the fair!
   Ⓓ I just love this book so much?

2. Ⓐ That program was awful?
   Ⓑ Could you hear her sing!
   Ⓒ Let me watch for them.
   Ⓓ Ouch. That hurt.

In which sentence are commas used correctly?

3. Ⓐ I called, but Amy wasn't home.
   Ⓑ We ate cheese, apples and bread.
   Ⓒ "No" she said "I, can't go."
   Ⓓ The answer is, that we just don't know.

4. Ⓐ Stop look, and listen Bob.
   Ⓑ "We would like to go," said Hans.
   Ⓒ Enrique, my friend lives, in Houston.
   Ⓓ My arm hurts but, it's okay.

5. Ⓐ My best friend, Pat and I can come.
   Ⓑ Tell me now, what you want.
   Ⓒ Well, yes, I do like spinach.
   Ⓓ I left and then, Karen went home.

In which sentence are quotation marks used correctly?

6. Ⓐ "No," said Tom, "I can't go.
   Ⓑ "Are you leaving?" asked Lee.
   Ⓒ "Yes, said Joe, I am."
   Ⓓ Carol said, Be sure to write!"

7. Ⓐ Brent said, "Throw that away."
   Ⓑ "It's still good, said Rebecca."
   Ⓒ "Now," said Lily, just watch me!"
   Ⓓ "Don't forget to jump, said Ruth.

In which phrase are colons used correctly?

8. Ⓐ Dear Mom:
   Ⓑ Sincerely yours:
   Ⓒ 10:30 P.M.
   Ⓓ 615 A.M.

In which sentence are apostrophes used correctly?

9. Ⓐ I ca'nt meet you until 6:30.
   Ⓑ Il'l walk the dog.
   Ⓒ It's 12:00, and I am late!
   Ⓓ The dog shook it's head.

10. Ⓐ I'm sorry I can't be there.
    Ⓑ Lets' go together.
    Ⓒ I need two day's notice.
    Ⓓ Were all staying home.

Nouns

Directions Darken the circle for the kind of noun that is underlined in each sentence.

1. The judge told <u>Mr. Clark</u> he was free to go.   Ⓐ common Ⓑ proper Ⓒ possessive

2. Our <u>vacation</u> was wonderful.   Ⓐ common Ⓑ proper Ⓒ possessive

3. My <u>brother's</u> ranch is in Wyoming.   Ⓐ common Ⓑ proper Ⓒ possessive

Directions Darken the circle for the correct form of the noun.

4. plural   Ⓐ horse   Ⓑ horses   Ⓒ horse's

5. possessive   Ⓐ brush   Ⓑ brush's   Ⓒ brushes

6. singular   Ⓐ men   Ⓑ man   Ⓒ men's

Directions Write a proper noun suggested by each common noun.

7. singer _____   10. car _____

8. holiday _____   11. month _____

9. city   _____   12. state _____

Directions Write a common noun suggested by each proper noun.

13. Nile   _____   16. Mexico _____

14. Jupiter _____   17. Sahara _____

15. Susan   _____   15. Honolulu _____

Name _____ Date _____

Verbs

Directions Darken the circle for the verb(s) that correctly completes each sentence.

1. Can you ____ me how to play the guitar? Ⓐ learn Ⓑ learned Ⓒ teach

2. He said he ____ want any meat. Ⓐ don't Ⓑ doesn't Ⓒ do

3. I am going to ____ down now. Ⓐ lie Ⓑ lay Ⓒ lying

4. Jason ____ need anything from the store. Ⓐ do Ⓑ doesn't Ⓒ don't

5. I ____ waiting on her for an hour. Ⓐ been Ⓑ had Ⓒ have been

6. ____ I have your new phone number? Ⓐ May Ⓑ Does Ⓒ Can

7. Will Joan have time to ____ down before lunch? Ⓐ lie Ⓑ set Ⓒ lay

8. Please ____ the book on the table. Ⓐ lie Ⓑ set Ⓒ sit

9. ____ Carol going to pick up her package? Ⓐ Are Ⓑ Were Ⓒ Is

10. She wants to ____ how to ski. Ⓐ learns Ⓑ learned Ⓒ learn

11. Did Kurt tell you that these ____ his photographs? Ⓐ was Ⓑ is Ⓒ are

12. He ____ work at the library this year. Ⓐ don't Ⓑ doesn't Ⓒ doing

13. She ____ speak if there is time. Ⓐ may Ⓑ was Ⓒ is

14. It takes time to ____ something new. Ⓐ learn Ⓑ teached Ⓒ taught

15. We ____ to the park for lunch. Ⓐ gone Ⓑ went Ⓒ have went

16. She ____ out her old clothes. Ⓐ throw Ⓑ thrown Ⓒ threw

17. Sylvia ____ her a present. Ⓐ gived Ⓑ gave Ⓒ given

18. I ____ may favorite vase yesterday. Ⓐ broke Ⓑ had broke Ⓒ broken

19. The bottle of soda ____. Ⓐ freezed Ⓑ frozed Ⓒ froze

20. Who ____ this story? Ⓐ wrote Ⓑ write Ⓒ written

Pronouns

Directions Darken the circle for the pronoun that correctly completes each sentence.

1. Nina chose ____ as her partner?   Ⓐ whom   Ⓑ she   Ⓒ who

2. It was ____ who cooked the turkey.   Ⓐ her   Ⓑ we   Ⓒ us

3. Chuck gave the prettiest flower to ____.   Ⓐ she   Ⓑ hers   Ⓒ her

4. Please tell ____ to meet us at six o'clock.   Ⓐ them   Ⓑ their   Ⓒ they

5. ____ and Laurel are going to the concert tonight.   Ⓐ He   Ⓑ Him   Ⓒ Her

6. ____ was waiting for me when I got home.   Ⓐ They   Ⓑ Both   Ⓒ No one

7. Have you ever met ____ parents?   Ⓐ hers   Ⓑ their   Ⓒ them

8. Tobie's father is taking ____ on a camping trip.   Ⓐ we   Ⓑ they   Ⓒ him

9. You and ____ are the best dancers in our class.   Ⓐ them   Ⓑ their   Ⓒ they

10. Which jacket is ____?   Ⓐ your   Ⓑ hers   Ⓒ you're

11. Lucy and ____ are best friends.   Ⓐ she   Ⓑ her   Ⓒ them

12. The team held a car wash to raise money for ____ new uniforms.   Ⓐ they're   Ⓑ their   Ⓒ there

13. Jerry and ____ almost missed the bus this morning.   Ⓐ her   Ⓑ him   Ⓒ I

14. My grandmother baked cookies for Eddie and ____.   Ⓐ we   Ⓑ she   Ⓒ me

15. Mr. Sewell gave ____ books for our school library.   Ⓐ ourselves   Ⓑ our   Ⓒ us

16. My Mom's and ____ eyes are similar.   Ⓐ my's   Ⓑ my   Ⓒ I's

Using Words Correctly

Directions Darken the circle for the adjective or adverb that correctly completes each sentence.

1. This is the ____ ice cream I've ever had.

- Ⓐ smoother
- Ⓑ smoothest
- Ⓒ most smooth
- Ⓓ smoothier

2. A squirrel can run ____ than a dog.

- Ⓐ quickest
- Ⓑ quickly
- Ⓒ more quickly
- Ⓓ more quick

3. Of all the final exams I took last week, math was the ____.

- Ⓐ easier
- Ⓒ easiest
- Ⓑ most easy
- Ⓓ more easier

4. Flying is the ____ way to travel from city to city.

- Ⓐ more most expensive
- Ⓑ expensivest
- Ⓒ most expensivest
- Ⓓ most expensive

5. Who was the ____ player on the team?

- Ⓐ most best
- Ⓒ bestest
- Ⓑ more best
- Ⓓ best

6. That was the ____ movie I ever saw.

- Ⓐ funnier
- Ⓒ most funny
- Ⓑ funnest
- Ⓓ funniest

7. The instructions for driving to the park were really ____.

- Ⓐ clear
- Ⓒ clearest
- Ⓑ clearer
- Ⓓ more clearer

8. Our team is ____ in the standings than any other team in the league.

- Ⓐ higher
- Ⓒ high
- Ⓑ highest
- Ⓓ more high

9. Our class arrived ____ than the other classes because our bus broke down.

- Ⓐ latest
- Ⓒ more later
- Ⓑ later
- Ⓓ late

10. Of all the dogs we've owned, Ginger was the ____ to train.

- Ⓐ easier
- Ⓒ easiest
- Ⓑ most easier
- Ⓓ more easier

11. Jodi is the ____ person I know.

- Ⓐ cheerfulest
- Ⓒ more cheerful
- Ⓑ most cheerful
- Ⓓ cheerfuler

12. Our bus broke down, so our class arrived ____ than the other classes.

- Ⓐ latest
- Ⓒ lately
- Ⓑ later
- Ⓓ late

Sentence Parts

(Directions) Darken the circle for the correct answer.

1. What is the complete **subject** of this sentence?

No one else can do high jumps like Phil.

- (A) Phil
- (B) high jumps
- (C) No one else
- (D) can do

2. What is the complete **subject** of this sentence?

All of the students went to the track meet.

- (A) All of the students
- (B) the students
- (C) the track meet
- (D) track meet

3. What is the complete **predicate** of this sentence?

Everyone on the ship waved as we sailed away.

- (A) Everyone on the ship
- (B) the ship waved
- (C) waved as we sailed away
- (D) we sailed away

4. What is the complete **predicate** of this sentence?

Our school closes for winter recess.

- (A) Our school
- (B) closes for winter recess
- (C) school closes
- (D) winter recess

5. What is the complete **subject** of this sentence?

Our school has a new auditorium.

- (A) a new auditorium
- (B) has a new
- (C) Our school has
- (D) Our school

6. What is the complete **predicate** of this sentence?

Charles Dickens wrote many stories about life in London.

- (A) Charles Dickens
- (B) life in London
- (C) wrote many stories about life in London
- (D) Dickens wrote

7. What is the complete **subject** of this sentence?

George Washington is called the father of our country.

- (A) the father of our country
- (B) George Washington
- (C) our country
- (D) Washington is called

8. What is the complete **subject** of this sentence?

Our campsite was located near a lake.

- (A) near a lake
- (B) was located
- (C) Our campsite
- (D) Our campsite was located

Sentences

Directions Write **D** before the declarative sentence, **IM** before the imperative sentence, **E** before the exclamatory sentence, and **IN** before the interrogative sentence.

_____ **1.** Don't worry about a thing.

_____ **2.** It is best to just wait.

_____ **3.** Who is going with us?

_____ **4.** I feel awful!

Directions Write **CS** before the compound sentence. Write **RO** before the run-on sentence. Write **I** before the sentence that is in inverted order.

_____ **5.** We had been there once before, it was familiar to me.

_____ **6.** Around the corner sped the getaway car.

_____ **7.** Time was running out, and darkness was falling.

Directions Use the choices below to label each sentence.

    A compound   **B** simple   **C** complex   **D** fragment

_____ **8.** Juan is very unhappy because his best friend is moving.

_____ **9.** We need to buy more supplies, or we won't be able to finish the project.

_____ **10.** My favorite program.

_____ **11.** Who was the last one to use the scissors?

_____ **12.** Frank, who lives near me, is a good chess player.

_____ **13.** Sara Jean is only eleven, yet she can read her sister's high school books.

_____ **14.** The new computer, which they just bought, has a lot of good software.

_____ **15.** Anybody who plays tennis.

Spelling

Directions Darken the circle for the word that is spelled correctly.

1. We traced the ____ on a map.
   - (A) rout
   - (B) ruote
   - (C) roote
   - (D) route

2. Last week we had some warm ____.
   - (A) wethar
   - (B) wethare
   - (C) weather
   - (D) waether

3. The house is ____ by beautiful trees.
   - (A) surounded
   - (B) surrounded
   - (C) serrounded
   - (D) sarrounded

4. Come ____ home after school.
   - (A) striaght
   - (B) straight
   - (C) straihgt
   - (D) straitgh

5. Another word for closet is ____.
   - (A) cupbord
   - (B) cubboard
   - (C) cupboard
   - (D) cuboard

6. Rocco bought new skates, ____ he didn't need them.
   - (A) although
   - (B) allthough
   - (C) althogh
   - (D) althow

7. Carla was ____ for the help Nat gave her.
   - (A) greatful
   - (B) graetful
   - (C) gratefull
   - (D) grateful

8. My dad wants to buy camping ____.
   - (A) eqwipment
   - (B) equipment
   - (C) equepment
   - (D) eqwepment

9. I forgot to write down tonight's homework ____.
   - (A) assignment
   - (B) asinment
   - (C) assinment
   - (D) assignmint

10. I wonder who will be ____ of the debating team.
    - (A) captin
    - (B) captine
    - (C) captain
    - (D) captein

11. Lorena paid a ____ price for the popular toy.
    - (A) bargin
    - (B) bargan
    - (C) bargain
    - (D) bargine

12. Use a sponge to ____ the water on the floor.
    - (A) assorb
    - (B) abzorb
    - (C) absorb
    - (D) asbourb

Spelling

Directions Darken the circle for the letter of the phrase that has a misspelled underlined word.

1. Ⓐ <u>muscle</u> tone
   Ⓑ <u>exercize</u> room
   Ⓒ <u>heroes'</u> welcome
   Ⓓ <u>writing</u> assignment

2. Ⓐ work <u>togehther</u>
   Ⓑ <u>business</u> card
   Ⓒ <u>tomorrow</u> morning
   Ⓓ <u>whole</u> group

3. Ⓐ <u>always</u> win
   Ⓑ good <u>enough</u>
   Ⓒ <u>arithmitic</u> test
   Ⓓ <u>already</u> knew that

4. Ⓐ soccer <u>tournament</u>
   Ⓑ green <u>vegetables</u>
   Ⓒ <u>rasberries</u> and cream
   Ⓓ <u>tomorrow</u> night

5. Ⓐ <u>transparrent</u> fabric
   Ⓑ <u>sugar</u> bowl
   Ⓒ <u>wrapping</u> paper
   Ⓓ science <u>experiment</u>

6. Ⓐ <u>balloon</u> tire
   Ⓑ <u>your</u> the one
   Ⓒ <u>busy</u> workers
   Ⓓ new <u>calendar</u>

7. Ⓐ <u>listen</u> carefully
   Ⓑ give <u>advice</u>
   Ⓒ piano <u>lessons</u>
   Ⓓ <u>remmember</u> the date

8. Ⓐ <u>libary</u> book
   Ⓑ <u>across</u> the road
   Ⓒ <u>sometime</u> later
   Ⓓ <u>ready</u> to go

9. Ⓐ guarantee <u>satisfacktion</u>
   Ⓑ cheese <u>sandwich</u>
   Ⓒ traffic <u>signal</u>
   Ⓓ essay <u>question</u>

10. Ⓐ <u>question</u> mark
    Ⓑ <u>raging</u> storm
    Ⓒ <u>hurrecane</u> winds
    Ⓓ <u>reverse</u> order

11. Ⓐ stage <u>scenery</u>
    Ⓑ <u>research</u> paper
    Ⓒ <u>magazine</u> story
    Ⓓ <u>leoperd</u> sports

12. Ⓐ <u>pleasent</u> memory
    Ⓑ defense <u>lawyer</u>
    Ⓒ oil <u>paint</u>
    Ⓓ principal's <u>office</u>

Spelling

Directions Learn to spell these words. Use each word in a sentence.
Spell these words correctly in all your writing.

a lot	collect	expect	laid	prepare	surely
absence	compare	fierce	latter	principal	surprise
ache	cough	finally	library	principle	terrible
achieve	could	first	lightning	proceed	their
address	couldn't	flies	likely	pursue	there
adjust	country	fourth	little	quarter	therefore
advice	county	friend	loose	quiet	they
advise	cousin	getting	lose	quite	they'll
again	crowd	grateful	losing	raise	thief
all right	cruel	grieve	making	really	though
almost	deceive	guard	maybe	receipt	thought
along	defense	guess	meant	receive	through
already	dependent	guessed	million	recipe	tired
although	descend	guest	minute	recommend	tomorrow
among	describe	handle	neither	referring	toward
answered	desert	haven't	niece	remain	trouble
aunt	desperate	having	none	remember	truly
autumn	dessert	heard	occasion	repetition	unusual
awhile	didn't	height	occur	respect	using
balloon	diet	hello	often	rhythm	usually
because	difference	herd	omitted	right	vacuum
been	different	heroes	opinion	rough	valuable
before	disappear	hoping	outside	route	visible
beginning	dissatisfied	hour	paid	safety	wear
believe	distance	house	peace	salary	weigh
bought	doubt	hurrying	people	scene	weird
break	dropped	immediately	perhaps	schedule	whole
brought	early	impossible	personal	sense	woman
built	effect	instead	persuade	separate	wrench
busy	employ	interest	piece	several	write
calendar	enough	it's	planned	similar	writing
carrying	eventually	its	pleasant	sincerely	yacht
ceiling	exceed	judgment	please	skis	yield
chief	excellent	knew	possess	soon	you're
choose	except	knife	possible	special	your
chosen	exist	know	practice	straight	
close	exit	knowledge	prefer	succeed	

Reference Materials

Directions Darken the circle for the correct answer.

1. To find information for a report about John Adams, you would look in the ____.

  Ⓐ encyclopedia   Ⓒ dictionary

  Ⓑ atlas   Ⓓ newspaper

2. To find the address for the Jiffy Printing Company, you would look in the ____.

  Ⓐ encyclopedia   Ⓒ dictionary

  Ⓑ atlas   Ⓓ telephone directory

3. To find the main highways in the state of Texas, you would look in the ____.

  Ⓐ dictionary   Ⓒ newspaper

  Ⓑ atlas   Ⓓ telephone directory

4. To find the meaning of the word *extemporaneous*, you would look in the ____.

  Ⓐ dictionary   Ⓒ encyclopedia

  Ⓑ telephone directory Ⓓ atlas

5. To find the telephone number to call for Brighton Elementary School, you would look in the ____.

  Ⓐ dictionary   Ⓒ encyclopedia

  Ⓑ telephone directory Ⓓ newspaper

6. To find information about the Treaty of Ghent, you would look in the ____.

  Ⓐ newspaper   Ⓒ dictionary

  Ⓑ telephone directory Ⓓ encyclopedia

7. To find the way to pronounce the word *melee*, you would look in the ____.

  Ⓐ encyclopedia   Ⓒ newspaper

  Ⓑ dictionary   Ⓓ atlas

8. To find the history of the word *coyote*, you would look in the ____.

  Ⓐ newspaper   Ⓒ telephone directory

  Ⓑ atlas   Ⓓ dictionary

Parts of a Book

Directions Use the sample book pages to answer questions 1–5.
Write the letter that represents the page that contains the answer.

AFRICA A Land of Empires by Dorothy J. Morgan LANDMARK PUBLICATIONS Chicago New York Toronto	Copyright © 1985 by Landmark Publications **Acknowledgments** *Millburn Publishing Company:* "Watusi Legends" from *African Literature,* ed. by R.R. Adams. Copyright © 1967. *Tifford, Inc.* "Sunset" from *Poetry Monthly,* October 1981. All rights reserved. Printed in the United States of America.	**CONTENTS** 1. The Africa of the Romans ... 1 2. The Sarakole Empire .... 25 3. The Mali Empire .... 53 4. The Ethiopian Empire ...... 75 5. The Baguirimi Empire ...... 153 Glossary .... 175 Index 187
Ⓐ **title page**	Ⓑ **copyright page**	Ⓒ **table of contents**

1. How many chapters does the book contain? _____

2. On which page does the chapter about the Mali Empire begin? _____

3. When and where was the book published? _____

4. Who wrote the book? _____

5. From which magazine did the author reprint a poem? _____

Af·ri·kaans (af′ri·käns′) *n.* One of the two official languages of present-day South Africa.
 an·tiq·ui·ty (an·tik′wə·tē) *n.*
 1 The quality of being very old.   **2** Ancient times, especially before the Middle Ages.
 ar·ti·fact (är′tə·fakt′) *n.* Anything made by human work or art.
	S
	
	 Sahara, 12–13, 19, 45
	 Sarakole peoples, 36, 40–44
	 Senegal, 8, 24, 103
	 Sierra Leone, 5, 26, 71
	 Songhay, 7, 13, 25, 120
	   liberation from Mali, 108
	   peoples, 105–108, 125–130
	   reign of Sonni Ali, 135–139
	   split, 150, 152–153

glossary	**index**

Directions Use the glossary and index sample to answer questions 6–8.

6. How many syllables does *Afrikaans* have? _____

7. What part of speech is *antiquity*? _____

8. On which pages would you find information about Sonni Ali? _____

Dictionary Skills

Directions Refer to the dictionary samples to answer questions 1–6.
Darken the circle for the correct answer.

---

leav-en (lev´en) *n.* **1.** a substance that causes dough to rise. **2.** a small piece of such dough put aside to be used for causing other dough to rise. *-v.* to cause dough to rise. [Middle English, from Old French, from Latin *levein*.]
left (left) *adj.* toward the side of the body that is westward when

facing north. *-n.* that is on the left. *-adv.* toward the left. [Middle English *lift*, from Old English *lyft*, weak.]
let (let) *v.* **1.** to permit or allow: *Did he let you go?* **2.** to allow to pass through: *I let the bird out of its cage.* **3.** to make; cause: *They'll let us know.* **4.** to rent. [Old English *laeten*, to allow.]

---

1. As which part of speech can <u>left</u> not be used?

    Ⓐ pronoun   Ⓑ adjective   Ⓒ adverb

2. Which word originally meant "weak"?

    Ⓐ let   Ⓑ left   Ⓒ leaven

3. From how many other languages did <u>leaven</u> come?

    Ⓐ two   Ⓑ three   Ⓒ four

4. Which word has the most definitions?

    Ⓐ leaven   Ⓑ let   Ⓒ left

5. Which pair of words could be guide words for the entries above?

    Ⓐ leaf/level   Ⓑ lay/lean   Ⓒ length/liar

6. Which word has two syllables?

    Ⓐ leaven   Ⓑ left   Ⓒ let

---

a	add	i	it	o͞o	took	oi	oil
ā	ace	ī	ice	o͞o	pool	ou	pout
â	care	o	odd	u	up	ng	ring
ä	palm	ō	open	û	burn	th	thin
e	end	ô	order	yo͞o	fuse	th	this
ē	equal					zh	vision

ə = { a in *above*   e in *sicken*   i in *possible*
      o in *melon*   u in *circus* }

Directions Use the pronunciation key above to answer questions 7 and 8. Think about the pronunciation of each word. Then, darken the circle by the correct answer.

7. **hy•giene** [hī´jēn]

The last syllable in **hygiene** sounds like _____.

    Ⓐ gin   Ⓑ Jean   Ⓒ Jane

8. **pneu•mo•nia** [n(y)o͞o mōn´ yə]

The first syllable in **pneumonia** begins with the same sound as _____.

    Ⓐ pony   Ⓑ full   Ⓒ notice

Directions Read each pair of guide words and the list of entry words. Circle each entry word that would appear on the page.

9. **money/muscle**   museum   muddy   modest

10. **perfect/pin**   pit   pizza   pile

Charts and Graphs

(**Directions**) Use the chart below to find the answers. Darken the circle for the correct answer.

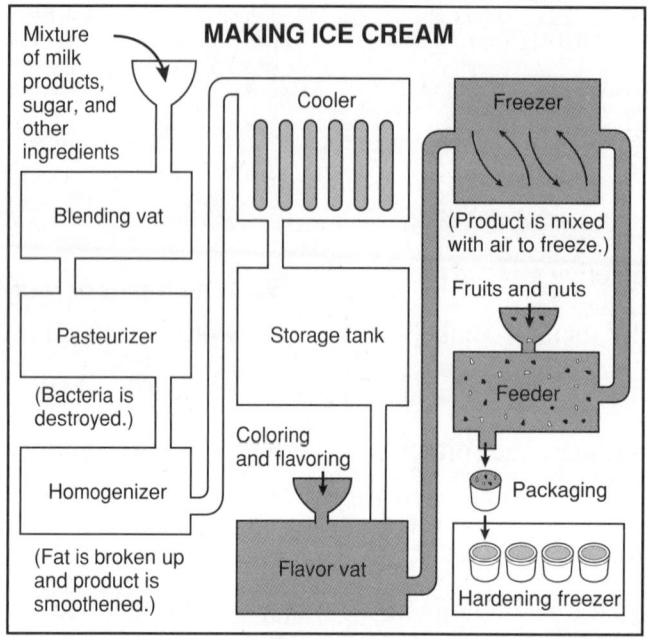

1. Where does the mixture go next after it leaves storage tank?

  Ⓐ   to the freezer
  Ⓑ   to the flavor vat
  Ⓒ   to the cooler
  Ⓓ   to the pasteurizer

2. Which happens first?

  Ⓐ   The ice cream goes into a hardening freezer.
  Ⓑ   The ice cream is homogenized.
  Ⓒ   Fruits and nuts are added.
  Ⓓ   The ingredients go into a blending vat.

3. What is the title of this chart?

  Ⓐ   Ice Cream Processing
  Ⓑ   Making Iced Milk
  Ⓒ   Making Ice Cream
  Ⓓ   Ice Cream Making

4. Where is the bacteria destroyed?

  Ⓐ   in the blending vat
  Ⓑ   in the homogenizer
  Ⓒ   in the storage tank
  Ⓓ   in the pasteurizer

5. When does the product go into the cooler?

  Ⓐ   after it is homogenized
  Ⓑ   after the coloring and flavoring are added
  Ⓒ   after it is packaged
  Ⓓ   right after it is blended

6. What is used to make the product freeze?

  Ⓐ   coloring and flavoring
  Ⓑ   fruits and nuts
  Ⓒ   air
  Ⓓ   milk products

Name _____ Date _____

Personal Narrative

Directions Read the personal narrative. Answer the following questions in complete sentences.

The family birthday party began as usual. First, my family gathered after dinner with my presents. I was excited, but I thought I knew what I was getting. My parents had never been able to surprise me.

After I had opened one gift, I heard a faint rustling noise. I paused for a moment, but I heard nothing more. A minute later, I noticed that a large box moved! It was creepy! I jumped to my feet in alarm.

Laughing, my father then picked up the moving present. The box had no bottom at all. A fluffy kitten was curled up where the present had been. I was finally surprised—with the best birthday present I had ever received.

1. How did the writer feel at the beginning of the narrative?

_____

_____

2. How did the writer's feelings change by the end of the narrative?

_____

3. From what point of view is this narrative told?

_____

_____

4. What words are clues to this point of view?

_____

5. On another sheet of paper, write your own personal narrative.

How-To Paragraph

Directions Read the how-to paragraph. Answer the questions.

Fooling Your Friends with Dishwater Punch

An April Fool's Day party can be fun. You can fool and surprise your friends by serving them this delicious punch. It looks like dishwater. Do not let your friends see you make the punch. You will need the following items:

- a bowl that holds at least three quarts
- a package of green drink mix
- one quart of orange juice

- one quart of lemon soda
- one pint of pineapple sherbet
- a large spoon

First, pour the orange juice into the bowl. Next, add the package of green drink mix. Stir it in. The juice should look grayish, like dishwater. Add the sherbet in small scoops. Stir the mixture briskly with a spoon until some of the sherbet is melted. Then, add the lemon soda. The punch should look like soapy dishwater.

Offer the punch to your friends and tell them it is dishwater. If none of them will try it, drink a glass yourself. When someone finally tries it, shout "April Fool!"

1. How many items are required?

_____

2. What is the first thing you do?

_____

3. What must you not allow your friend to see?

_____

4. On another sheet of paper, write your own how-to paragraph.

Comparison and Contrast Paragraph

Directions Read each paragraph. Label each comparison or contrast.

My two friends Lena and Taylor are different in many ways. Lena complains if she does not like something, and she argues if she disagrees with me. Taylor rarely complains or argues, so we almost never fight. But Lena is a more honest friend. She says exactly what she thinks or feels. In contrast, Taylor never says anything negative to me about things I have said or done. Instead, she may say something to someone else, and her comments often get back to me.

1. _____

My friends Lena and Taylor are alike in many ways. Both are intelligent, loyal, and helpful. Either can carry on a great conversation. Each has an excellent sense of humor, and they enjoy many of the same activities.

2. _____

Directions Use the paragraphs to answer the questions.

3. In what way are the two friends different? Explain one way.

_____

_____

_____

4. In what way are the two friends alike? Explain one way.

_____

_____

_____

5. On another sheet of paper, write your own paragraph of comparison or contrast.

Persuasive Paragraph

Directions Read this business letter. Then, answer the questions that follow.

J M

Kensington
London, England
December 21, 1846

Mr. Ebenezer Scrooge
Financial District
London, England

Dear Mr. Scrooge:

One of your employees, Bob Cratchit, has applied for work with us. Mr. Cratchit is a fine man, and I think you should think carefully before letting him go. First of all, Bob is very quick with numbers—a valuable trait in your type of work. Second, he is a very loyal worker. If it were not for his son, Tiny Tim, he would never think of leaving your firm. Third, Mr. Cratchit is willing to work very long hours for very little pay. I feel I am certain that you should see to this immediately. For some reason, I sense that it may be of great importance.

Sincerely,
James Martin

1. Write the topic sentence that states the opinion expressed in this letter.

_____

_____

_____

2. How many reasons does the writer give to support his opinion?

_____

3. What is the first reason given to support the opinion?

_____

_____

4. On another sheet of paper, write your own persuasive paragraph.

Descriptive Paragraph

(**Directions**) Read the descriptive paragraph. Answer the questions in complete sentences.

The room had clearly been ransacked. The drawers of the dresser next to the window were open and empty. A trail of assorted clothing led to the closet. The closet stood empty, its contents strewn across the bed and the floor. Glass from a broken perfume bottle crunched loudly underfoot, the fragrance of its contents mixing with the smell of the garlic. The only item left undisturbed was a portrait on the wall over the bed. Its subject, a solemn young woman, stared thoughtfully into the room. Estella could not believe the damage her new puppy had done!

1. What is the topic sentence of the paragraph?

_____

_____

2. Name a word or phrase that appeals to the sense of smell.

_____

_____

3. What phrase appeals to your sense of touch?

_____

_____

4. What are some words or paraphrases that the writer used to indicate space order?

_____

_____

5. On another sheet of paper, write your own descriptive paragraph.

Math Overall Assessment

Directions Darken the circle for the correct answer.

1. In the number 40,6̲25, in which place is the underlined digit?

- Ⓐ ten thousands
- Ⓒ thousands
- Ⓑ hundreds
- Ⓓ tens

2. 16% of 42 =

- Ⓐ 6.72
- Ⓒ 60.72
- Ⓑ 67.2
- Ⓓ 607.2

3. Which fraction equals $12\frac{1}{2}\%$?

- Ⓐ $\frac{2}{8}$
- Ⓒ $\frac{1}{4}$
- Ⓑ $\frac{3}{4}$
- Ⓓ $\frac{1}{8}$

4. $? - 4.6 = 1.7$

- Ⓐ 6.3
- Ⓒ 4.6
- Ⓑ 5.8
- Ⓓ 6.1

5. Which is the greatest decimal number?

- Ⓐ 0.1
- Ⓒ 0.28
- Ⓑ 0.205
- Ⓓ 0.135

6. What part of this graph tells about maple leaves?

- Ⓐ $\frac{1}{2}$
- Ⓑ $\frac{2}{3}$
- Ⓒ $\frac{1}{3}$
- Ⓓ $\frac{1}{4}$

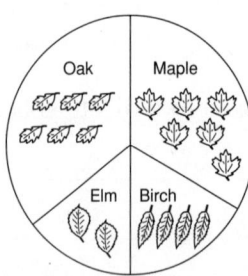

7. What number is missing from this pattern?

58, 52, _____, 40, 34

- Ⓐ 46
- Ⓒ 45
- Ⓑ 47
- Ⓓ 48

8.

PTA Income Sources

Fall Fiesta $41
Pizza Lunches $9
Book Fair $16
Market Day $24
Spring Plant Sale $10

What percent of PTA income comes from the Book Fair and Pizza Lunches?

- Ⓐ 25%
- Ⓒ 9%
- Ⓑ 16%
- Ⓓ 50%

9. $\frac{1}{3} + \frac{1}{6} =$

- Ⓐ $\frac{2}{9}$
- Ⓒ $\frac{1}{2}$
- Ⓑ $\frac{2}{6}$
- Ⓓ $\frac{1}{4}$

10. $\frac{5}{2} \times \frac{4}{3} =$

- Ⓐ $1\frac{9}{5}$
- Ⓒ $3\frac{1}{3}$
- Ⓑ $3\frac{7}{10}$
- Ⓓ $3\frac{1}{2}$

11. $3.12 \times 100 =$

- Ⓐ 312
- Ⓒ 3.120
- Ⓑ 31.20
- Ⓓ 0.312

12. $57 \div ? = 5.7$

- Ⓐ 1.0
- Ⓒ 10
- Ⓑ 1.07
- Ⓓ 100

13. If $125 + x = 550$, what is the value of x?

- Ⓐ 225
- Ⓒ 375
- Ⓑ 275
- Ⓓ 425

14. What is the standard way to write three and one hundred thirty-four thousandths?

- Ⓐ 3.034
- Ⓒ 3.134
- Ⓑ 3.304
- Ⓓ 3.0034

Math Overall Assessment, p. 2

Directions Darken the circle for the correct answer.

1. What is the least common denominator for this set of fractions?

$\frac{1}{3}$ $\frac{3}{4}$

- Ⓐ 4
- Ⓑ 12
- Ⓒ 3
- Ⓓ 7

2. What was the average temperature in degrees in Bay Town during June of 1992?

- Ⓐ 54
- Ⓑ 64
- Ⓒ 55
- Ⓓ 60

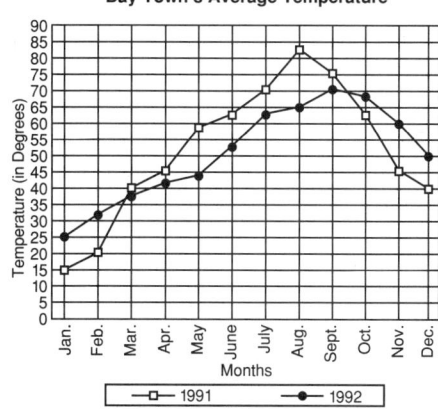

Bay Town's Average Temperature

3. What is the length of a rectangle with an area of 18 cm² and a width of 3 cm?

- Ⓐ 6 cm
- Ⓑ 9 cm
- Ⓒ 54 cm
- Ⓓ Not given

4. What is the probability of choosing a card with the letter A?

- Ⓐ $\frac{8}{10}$
- Ⓑ $\frac{1}{5}$
- Ⓒ $\frac{2}{5}$
- Ⓓ $\frac{4}{5}$

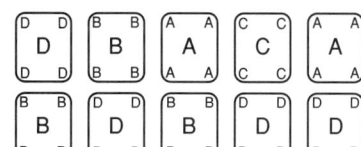

5. Jerome has one $10 bill, three $1 bills, one $5 bill, and six quarters. Vinnie has $6.35 more than Jerome. How much money does Vinnie have?

- Ⓐ $25.85
- Ⓑ $6.35
- Ⓒ $7.25
- Ⓓ $19.50

6. Harold is the sales manager of a CD company. He keeps a record of the number of cases of CDs the company sells each week. These are the weekly sales totals for the last 9 weeks: 39, 90, 95, 90, 92, 90, 94, 98, 95. What is the average number of cases of CD sales for this period?

- Ⓐ 87 cases
- Ⓑ 89 cases
- Ⓒ 92 cases
- Ⓓ 90 cases

7. There are 6 people in the Reed family. Each person takes a 5-minute shower every day. The family wants to conserve the amount of water they use when they take showers. They know that a standard showerhead uses about 6 gallons of water per minute. How many gallons of water does the family use to take showers each day?

- Ⓐ 30 gallons
- Ⓑ 180 gallons
- Ⓒ 1,250 gallons
- Ⓓ 60 gallons

8. If the Reed family purchases a showerhead that uses 3 gallons of water per minute, how many gallons of water will they save in a week?

- Ⓐ 1,350 gallons
- Ⓑ 630 gallons
- Ⓒ 620 gallons
- Ⓓ 15 gallons

Name _____   Date _____

Number Concepts

Directions Darken the circle for the correct answer.

1. Which is another sentence you can write about these numbers?

$9 + 4 = 13$ $4 + 9 = 13$

$13 - 9 = 4$ _____

- Ⓐ $9 - 4 = 5$
- Ⓑ $13 + 4 = 17$
- Ⓒ $13 - 4 = 9$
- Ⓓ $4 + 13 = 17$

2. Which is the Roman numeral for 1,562?

- Ⓐ MLCDII
- Ⓒ MCDVII
- Ⓑ MDLXII
- Ⓓ MCDVIII

3. Which represents $9,000 + 200 + 80 + 3$?

- Ⓐ 9,238
- Ⓒ 9,382
- Ⓑ 9,283
- Ⓓ 9,388

4. How would you write the standard form of six thousand, seven hundred thirty-six?

- Ⓐ 6,70036
- Ⓒ 60,736
- Ⓑ 6,367
- Ⓓ 6,736

5. What is the least number you can write using the digits 3, 2, 1, 8?

- Ⓐ 2,138
- Ⓒ 1,238
- Ⓑ 3,218
- Ⓓ 1,382

6. Which of these has a 4 in the ten-thousands place?

- Ⓐ 367,523
- Ⓒ 2,354,972
- Ⓑ 46,578
- Ⓓ 4,724

7. Which is not a factor of 4?

- Ⓐ 2
- Ⓒ 1
- Ⓑ 4
- Ⓓ 6

8. Which are the factors of the prime number 3?

- Ⓐ 1, 3
- Ⓒ 3, 0
- Ⓑ 1, 2
- Ⓓ 0, 0

9. Which answer shows counting by threes?

- Ⓐ 5, 8, 11, 14
- Ⓒ 3, 5, 8, 10
- Ⓑ 6, 9, 13, 7
- Ⓓ 2, 4, 6, 8

10. What letter goes in the box to make this sentence true?

$(d \times e) \times f = d \times (\square \times f)$

- Ⓐ f
- Ⓒ x
- Ⓑ d
- Ⓓ e

11. Which is a true sentence?

- Ⓐ $6,238 > 6,823$
- Ⓑ $4,801 > 4,892$
- Ⓒ $9,321 < 10,124$
- Ⓓ $962 < 729$

12. Which is the smallest common factor of 8 and 12?

- Ⓐ 4
- Ⓒ 2
- Ⓑ 1
- Ⓓ 8

Number Concepts

Directions Darken the circle for the correct answer.

1. Name 100 more than 945.

Ⓐ 955   Ⓒ 1,045
Ⓑ 1,945   Ⓓ 1,145

2. What are the prime factors of 18?

Ⓐ 2 and 9   Ⓒ 2 and 3
Ⓑ 3 and 6   Ⓓ 9 and 6

3. Which of these is an odd number?

Ⓐ 419   Ⓒ 812
Ⓑ 654   Ⓓ 400

4. What number is missing from this pattern?

67, 62, 57, _____, 47

Ⓐ 72   Ⓒ 52
Ⓑ 42   Ⓓ 27

5. Which number sentence is *not* true?

Ⓐ 290 > 1390   Ⓒ 9 < 10
Ⓑ 875 < 888   Ⓓ 29 > 24

6. Which are common multiples of 3 and 4?

Ⓐ 6 and 8   Ⓒ 12 and 6
Ⓑ 8 and 12   Ⓓ 12 and 24

7. Which of these is equal to 12?

Ⓐ 12 + 1   Ⓒ 12 × 12
Ⓑ 12 × 1   Ⓓ 12 × 0

8. What number makes both of these sentences true?

$0 \div 3 = \square$

$\square \times 9 = 0$

Ⓐ 9   Ⓒ 1
Ⓑ 0   Ⓓ 3

9. Choose the operation that makes this number sentence true.

$4 \times 5 = (9 + 13) \; \square \; 2$

Ⓐ +   Ⓒ ×
Ⓑ −   Ⓓ ÷

10. Which are two factors of 12?

Ⓐ 6 and 8   Ⓒ 3 and 4
Ⓑ 7 and 4   Ⓓ 5 and 6

11. In the number 435,562, what number does the underlined digit name?

Ⓐ 500   Ⓒ 50
Ⓑ 5,000   Ⓓ 50,000

12. Which are the prime factors of 6?

Ⓐ 3 and 3   Ⓒ 2 and 3
Ⓑ 0 and 2   Ⓓ 6 and 6

Addition and Subtraction of Whole Numbers

Directions Darken the circle for the correct answer.

1.   1,017
       + 3,438

   (A) 4,355   (C) 4,455
   (B) 5,455   (D) 4,555

2.   4,780
       5,791
         208
     + 3,054

   (A) 13,933   (C) 13,833
   (B) 12,833   (D) 13,634

3. $15.62
       + 4.17

   (A) $20.79   (C) $19.89
   (B) $19.79   (D) $20.69

4. 136 + 396 =

   (A) 422   (C) 432
   (B) 532   (D) 542

5.   70,951
       −   540

   (A) 70,011   (C) 74,011
   (B) 70,411   (D) 70,410

6. 3,527 + 4,664 =

   (A) 7,181   (C) 7,201
   (B) 8,191   (D) 8,181

7. 146 + ? + 97 = 523

   (A) 300   (C) 200
   (B) 400   (D) 280

8.   8,010
       − 3,762

   (A) 4,248   (C) 4,258
   (B) 5,248   (D) 4,238

9.   83,019
       − 71,821

   (A) 12,198   (C) 14,198
   (B) 11,188   (D) 11,198

10. ? − 38 = 91

   (A) 139   (C) 120
   (B) 129   (D) 130

Multiplication and Division of Whole Numbers

Directions Darken the circle for the correct answer.

1. 207
  × 8

   Ⓐ 1,087
   Ⓑ 1,656
   Ⓒ 10,656
   Ⓓ Not given

2. 14
  × 23

   Ⓐ 321
   Ⓑ 37
   Ⓒ 322
   Ⓓ Not given

3. $732 \times 4 =$

   Ⓐ 738
   Ⓑ 2,928
   Ⓒ 1,928
   Ⓓ Not given

4. $14 \times 14 =$

   Ⓐ 60
   Ⓑ 186
   Ⓒ 198
   Ⓓ 196

5. $25\overline{)780}$

   Ⓐ 30 R 3
   Ⓑ 31
   Ⓒ 31 R 5
   Ⓓ Not given

6. $34\overline{)73,916}$

   Ⓐ 2,174
   Ⓑ 6,234
   Ⓒ 2,674
   Ⓓ Not given

7. $32\overline{)9,408}$

   Ⓐ 295
   Ⓑ 293 R 21
   Ⓒ 293 R 26
   Ⓓ 294

8. $705 \text{ R } 8 = ? \div 32$

   Ⓐ 21,568
   Ⓑ 22,568
   Ⓒ 21,570
   Ⓓ Not given

9. $37 \div 2 =$

   Ⓐ 18
   Ⓑ 17 R 2
   Ⓒ 18 R 1
   Ⓓ Not given

10. $70 \times 36 =$

   Ⓐ 2,520
   Ⓑ 2,502
   Ⓒ 2,420
   Ⓓ Not given

Geometry

Directions Darken the circle for the correct answer.

1. Which line is a chord?

Ⓐ CB
Ⓑ AB
Ⓒ CD

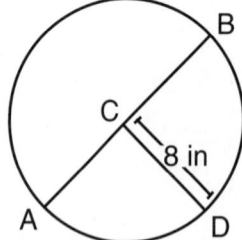

2. What is the measure of angle CBD on this protractor?

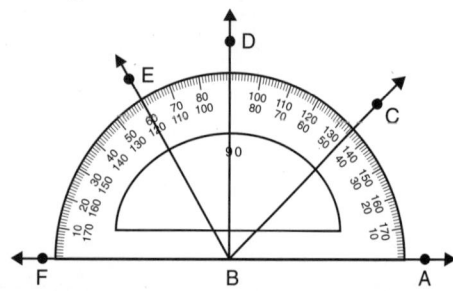

Ⓐ 120°
Ⓑ 90°
Ⓒ 45°

3. Which of these name parallel segments?

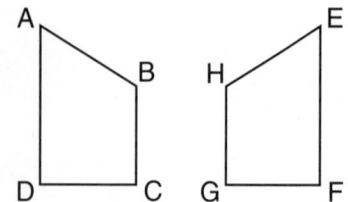

Ⓐ AB and CD
Ⓑ HG and EF
Ⓒ DC and BC

4. Which pair of lines is perpendicular?

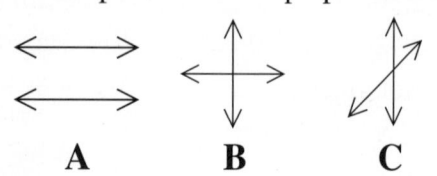

Ⓐ A
Ⓑ B
Ⓒ C

5. Which triangle shows a line of symmetry?

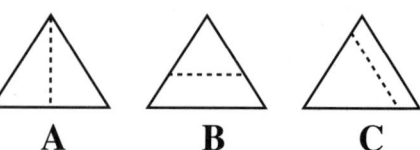

Ⓐ A
Ⓑ B
Ⓒ C

6. Which of these is an obtuse angle?

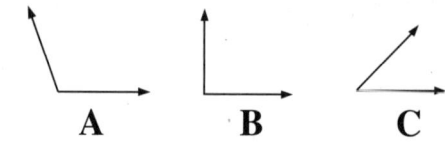

Ⓐ A
Ⓑ B
Ⓒ C

7. Which shapes are congruent?

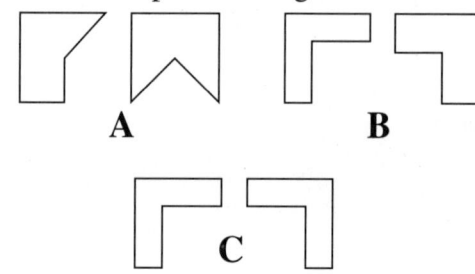

Ⓐ A
Ⓑ B
Ⓒ C

8. Which of these figures is a cylinder?

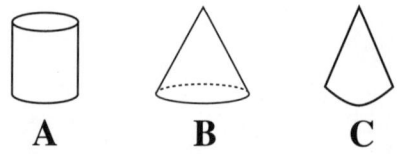

Ⓐ A
Ⓑ B
Ⓒ C

Measurement

Directions Darken the circle for the correct answer.

1. Which is used to measure liquid capacity?

- Ⓐ grams
- Ⓑ meters
- Ⓒ pounds
- Ⓓ liters

2. Which is another way to describe 4 quarts?

- Ⓐ $\frac{1}{2}$ gallon
- Ⓑ 1 gallon
- Ⓒ 6 pints
- Ⓓ Not given

3. How many *quarts* are in 8 cups?

- Ⓐ 4
- Ⓑ 3
- Ⓒ 2
- Ⓓ 1

4. 1,000 meters =

- Ⓐ 100 centimeters
- Ⓑ 1 kilometer
- Ⓒ 1 kilogram
- Ⓓ 1 liter

5. 1 liter =

- Ⓐ 1,000 grams
- Ⓑ 1,000 milliliters
- Ⓒ 1,000 millimeters
- Ⓓ 1,000 milligrams

6. How many cups of liquid would equal 16 ounces?

- Ⓐ 1 cup
- Ⓑ 2 cups
- Ⓒ 4 cups
- Ⓓ Not given

7. The height of a building is best expressed in _____.

- Ⓐ meters
- Ⓑ grams
- Ⓒ liters
- Ⓓ degrees

8. Which of these equals the greatest amount of liquid?

- Ⓐ 1 gallon
- Ⓑ 2 quarts
- Ⓒ 3 pints
- Ⓓ 4 cups

9. Ivan was sick for 24 hours. How long was Ivan sick?

- Ⓐ 1 month
- Ⓑ 1 second
- Ⓒ 1 minute
- Ⓓ 1 day

10. If a piece of string measures 12 centimeters, what is the equivalent in millimeters?

- Ⓐ 120 mm
- Ⓑ 6 mm
- Ⓒ 110 mm
- Ⓓ Not given

Name _____   Date _____

Fractions

Directions Darken the circle for the correct answer.

1. Which fraction means the same as $\frac{8}{12}$?

Ⓐ $\frac{1}{2}$ Ⓒ $\frac{3}{4}$

Ⓑ $\frac{2}{3}$ Ⓓ $\frac{5}{6}$

2. Which mixed number equals the improper fraction $\frac{20}{7}$?

Ⓐ $3\frac{1}{7}$ Ⓒ $4\frac{1}{7}$

Ⓑ $2\frac{5}{7}$ Ⓓ $2\frac{6}{7}$

3. In which two pictures are the same portion of squares shaded?

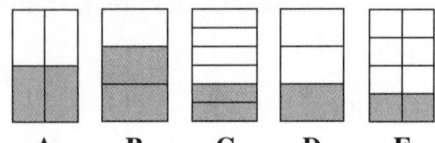

    A   **B**   **C**   **D**   **E**

Ⓐ A and B   Ⓒ C and D

Ⓑ B and C   Ⓓ B and E

4. $\frac{1}{4}$

    $\times\ 8$

Ⓐ $\frac{1}{2}$ Ⓒ 2

Ⓑ 4   Ⓓ 3

5. $\frac{1}{3}+\frac{2}{6}=$

Ⓐ $\frac{2}{9}$ Ⓒ $\frac{2}{3}$

Ⓑ $\frac{2}{6}$ Ⓓ $\frac{1}{9}$

6. What is the simplest form for $\frac{15}{30}$?

Ⓐ $\frac{1}{2}$ Ⓒ $\frac{5}{10}$

Ⓑ $\frac{3}{6}$ Ⓓ $\frac{5}{610}$

7. Which of these sentences is true?

Ⓐ $\frac{9}{12} < \frac{8}{12}$

Ⓑ $\frac{25}{60} > \frac{36}{60}$

Ⓒ $\frac{7}{10} = \frac{21}{30}$

Ⓓ $\frac{4}{15} = \frac{12}{30}$

8. What is the least common denominator for this set of fractions?

$\frac{7}{10}$ $\frac{2}{3}$

Ⓐ 30   Ⓒ 3

Ⓑ 10   Ⓓ 13

9. $\frac{13}{14}$

   $-\ \frac{3}{7}$

Ⓐ $\frac{1}{2}$ Ⓒ $\frac{2}{7}$

Ⓑ $\frac{1}{7}$ Ⓓ $\frac{10}{7}$

10. $\frac{6}{11} \div \frac{3}{8} =$

Ⓐ $3\frac{5}{8}$ Ⓒ $2\frac{5}{1}$

Ⓑ $1\frac{5}{1}$ Ⓓ $2\frac{1}{2}$

Decimals

Directions Darken the circle for the correct answer.

1. Four and three hundred three thousandths is written ____.

   (A) 4.330   (C) 4.303

   (B) 4.030   (D) 43.30

2. $0.0405 + 0.602 =$

   (A) 0.605   (C) 0.6425

   (B) 0.1007   (D) 0.06425

3. $0.762 - 0.471 =$

   (A) 0.299   (C) 303

   (B) 0.291   (D) 2.91

4. $0.9 \times 0.8 =$

   (A) 7.2   (C) 07.2

   (B) 0.72   (D) 0.072

5.   0.68

   $\times$ 0.4

   (A) 2.72   (C) 0.272

   (B) 0.270   (D) 2.072

6. $\$84.95 \div 17 =$

   (A) $4.99 R $0.12

   (B) $5.00

   (C) $49.92

   (D) $5.25

7. $12.62

   +   4.17

   (A) $16.79   (C) $17.79

   (B) $16.89   (D) $16.69

8. $\$3.40 - \$1.56 =$

   (A) $0.84   (C) $1.16

   (B) $1.84   (D) $2.06

9. Which number sentence is true?

   (A) $0.24 > 0.136$

   (B) $0.56 > 0.89$

   (C) $0.37 > 0.73$

   (D) $\$0.52 < \$0.46$

10. What is the place value of the 7 in this number? 8.007

   (A) ones   (C) hundredths

   (B) tens   (D) thousandths

11. $7.42 \div 100 =$

   (A) 0.0742   (C) 70.42

   (B) 1.742   (D) 0.742

12. Which fraction has the same value as 0.7?

   (A) $\frac{7}{10}$

   (B) $\frac{1}{7}$

   (C) $\frac{7}{7}$

   (D) $\frac{7}{100}$

Statistics and Probability

Directions Darken the circle for the correct answer.

1. How many students like to go biking in warm weather?

Ⓐ 40
Ⓑ 35
Ⓒ 25
Ⓓ 30

Favorite Warm-Weather Activity of Students	
Tennis	☼ ☼ ◖
Swimming	☼ ☼ ☼ ☼
Golfing	☼ ◖
Biking	☼ ☼ ☼ ◖
Hiking	☼ ☼ ☼

Each ☼ stands for 10.

2. Which point on the grid is located by the ordered pair (3, 2)?

Ⓐ M
Ⓑ K
Ⓒ J
Ⓓ L

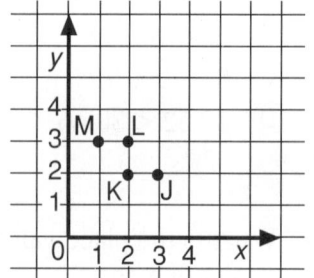

3. Each letter in the word *mathematics* is written on a card and placed in a box. If you choose a card without looking, what is probability that you will choose the letter *t*?

Ⓐ $\frac{1}{11}$ Ⓒ $\frac{3}{11}$

Ⓑ $\frac{2}{11}$ Ⓓ $\frac{4}{11}$

4. A bag contains 5 clear marbles and 10 colored marbles. What is the probability of reaching into the bag and pulling out a clear marble?

Ⓐ $\frac{10}{15}$ Ⓒ $\frac{5}{15}$

Ⓑ $\frac{7}{15}$ Ⓓ $\frac{3}{15}$

5. According to this table, how many drinks will you get from 6 cartons of apple juice?

Ⓐ 16
Ⓑ 24
Ⓒ 20
Ⓓ 22

Number of Drinks	
Number of Cartons of Apple Juice	Number of Drinks
2	8
3	12
4	16
5	?
6	?

6. What percent of class 6-B wrote book reports about adventure?

Ⓐ 30%
Ⓑ 40%
Ⓒ 10%
Ⓓ 20%

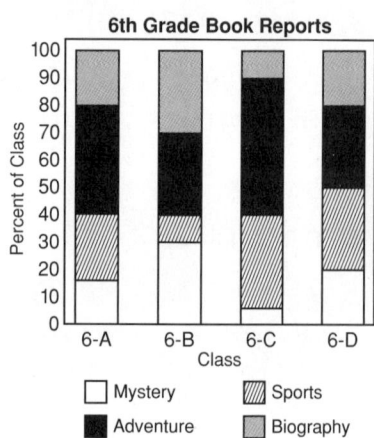

7. There are 4 red beads, 8 yellow beads, and 2 pink beads in a container. If 1 bead is picked at random from the container, what are the chances it will be red?

Ⓐ $\frac{2}{14}$ Ⓒ $\frac{6}{14}$

Ⓑ $\frac{4}{14}$ Ⓓ $\frac{8}{14}$

8. What is the probability of the spinner landing on 3?

Ⓐ $\frac{1}{2}$

Ⓑ $\frac{3}{8}$

Ⓒ $\frac{2}{3}$

Ⓓ $\frac{2}{8}$

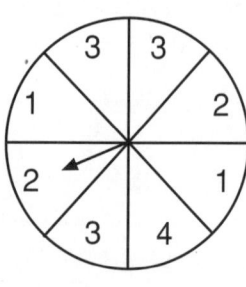

Pre-Algebra

Directions Darken the circle for the correct answer.

1. If $y = 54$, then $y \div 9 =$

Ⓐ 63
Ⓑ 45
Ⓒ 12
Ⓓ 6

2. If $y = 9$, then $y - 4 =$

Ⓐ 36
Ⓑ 13
Ⓒ 12
Ⓓ 5

3. If $y - 225 = 570$, then $y =$

Ⓐ 35
Ⓑ 235
Ⓒ 395
Ⓓ 795

4. If $x = 6$, then $x + 9 =$

Ⓐ 1
Ⓑ 10
Ⓒ 15
Ⓓ 18

5. If $30 - y = 22$, what is the value of y?

Ⓐ 52
Ⓑ 28
Ⓒ 12
Ⓓ 8

6. If $x \div 8 = 10$, then $x =$

Ⓐ 8
Ⓑ 16
Ⓒ 40
Ⓓ 80

7. If $x - 100 = 45$, then $x =$

Ⓐ 55
Ⓑ 145
Ⓒ 155
Ⓓ 255

8. If $175 + x = 350$, then $x =$

Ⓐ 125
Ⓑ 150
Ⓒ 175
Ⓓ 525

9. If $125 + x = 650$, then $x =$

Ⓐ 755
Ⓑ 625
Ⓒ 525
Ⓓ 475

10. If $27 \div y = 3$, then $y =$

Ⓐ 6
Ⓑ 12
Ⓒ 9
Ⓓ 18

Patterns

Directions Answer each question.

1. If you decided to begin to count at 2 with an increment of 1.5, what would the first five numbers of your sequence be?

_____ _____ _____ _____ _____

2. Darken the circle for each arithmetic sequence.

Ⓐ 3.2, 6.4, 9.6, 12.8, 16, …

Ⓑ 25, 22, 19, 16, 13, …

Ⓒ 1.3 + 1.2, 1.3 + 1.2 + 1.3, 1.3 + 1.2 + 1.3 + 1.2 …

Ⓓ 2.5, 2.5, 2.5, 2.5, …

Ⓔ $6, \frac{24}{2}, \frac{54}{3}, \frac{120}{5}, \frac{180}{6}, …$

3. Darken the circle for each geometric sequence.

Ⓐ 2, 6, 9, 14, …

Ⓑ 9,375; 1,875; 375; 75; 15; …

Ⓒ 7, 14, 28, 56, 112, …

Ⓓ 4, 8, 12, 16, 20, …

Directions Use the following set to answer questions 4 and 5.

$A = \{1, 3, 5, 7, 9, 11\}$

4. What is the ordinal of 3? _____

5. What is the ordinal of 9? _____

Directions Use the following sets to answer questions 6–9.

$C = \{3, 6, 9, 12, 15, 18, 21\}$ $G = \{1, 47\}$

$E = \{1; 11; 111; 1,111; 11,111\}$ $Q = \{2, 3, 5, 6, 8, 9\}$

6. What is the cardinality of Set G? _____

8. What is the ordinal of 5 in Set Q? _____

7. What is C_4? _____

9. What is the cardinality of Set E? _____

Ratio and Percent

Directions Darken the circle for the correct answer.

1. Change $\frac{9}{25}$ to a percent.

   Ⓐ 25%   Ⓒ 36%

   Ⓑ 9%   Ⓓ Not given

2. What is the fraction for 32%

   Ⓐ $\frac{5}{8}$ Ⓒ $\frac{32}{50}$

   Ⓑ $\frac{32}{100}$ Ⓓ $\frac{10}{21}$

3. Which ratio shows how many squares are shaded in this chart?

   Ⓐ 60:90

   Ⓑ 58:100

   Ⓒ 42:58

   Ⓓ 42:100

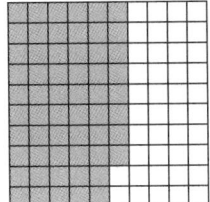

4. Change $\frac{4}{9}$ to a percent.

   Ⓐ 40%

   Ⓑ 44.4%

   Ⓒ 45%

   Ⓓ 49%

5. What percent of this pie is not shaded?

   Ⓐ 80%

   Ⓑ 20%

   Ⓒ 60%

   Ⓓ 33%

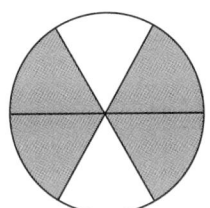

6. Which fraction expresses the ratio of 26 students to 1 teacher?

   Ⓐ $\frac{1}{26}$ Ⓒ $\frac{26}{1}$

   Ⓑ $\frac{26}{26}$ Ⓓ Not given

7. Which percent is another way to write $\frac{3}{80}$?

   Ⓐ $3\frac{1}{4}\%$ Ⓒ $4\frac{1}{4}\%$

   Ⓑ $3\frac{3}{4}\%$ Ⓓ $4\frac{1}{3}\%$

8. Which of these equals the decimal equivalent of 50%?

   Ⓐ 0.050

   Ⓑ 0.50

   Ⓒ 0.005

   Ⓓ 5.00

9. Change $\frac{2}{3}$ to a percent.

   Ⓐ $33\frac{1}{3}\%$

   Ⓑ $37\frac{1}{2}\%$

   Ⓒ $66\frac{2}{3}\%$

   Ⓓ $43\frac{3}{4}\%$

10. What is the decimal of 9%?

   Ⓐ 0.09

   Ⓑ 0.009

   Ⓒ 0.9

   Ⓓ 9.0

Math: Ratio and Percent

Assessments to Identify Skills and Needs 6, SV 3397-9

Estimation

Directions Darken the circle for the correct answer.

1. Round 517 to the nearest hundred.

Ⓐ 500
Ⓑ 400
Ⓒ 600
Ⓓ Not given

2. What is the closest estimate of 32×28?

Ⓐ 900
Ⓑ 850
Ⓒ 1,000
Ⓓ Not given

3. The closest estimate of 42×28 is ____.

Ⓐ 2,200
Ⓑ 1,400
Ⓒ 1,200
Ⓓ Not given

4. The closest estimate of $18.15 − $3.27 is ____.

Ⓐ $14
Ⓑ $15
Ⓒ $16
Ⓓ Not given

5. The closest estimate of $1,800 \div 800$ is between ____.

Ⓐ 4 and 5
Ⓑ 2 and 3
Ⓒ 1 and 2
Ⓓ Not given

6. Estimate the sum of 179 and 490.

Ⓐ 679
Ⓑ 800
Ⓒ 500
Ⓓ 700

7. Round 6,239 to the nearest thousand.

Ⓐ 5,000
Ⓑ 7,000
Ⓒ 6,000
Ⓓ Not given

8. Which number would be 40 if rounded to the nearest ten?

Ⓐ 32
Ⓑ 37
Ⓒ 29
Ⓓ Not given

9. Round the numbers to the nearest thousand. Then add.

  8,954
+ 1,853

Ⓐ 10,000
Ⓑ 7,000
Ⓒ 10,500
Ⓓ 11,000

10. Round 26,394 to the nearest thousand.

Ⓐ 27,000
Ⓑ 26,000
Ⓒ 28,000
Ⓓ Not given

Problem Solving: Whole Numbers

Directions Darken the circle for the correct answer.

1. Valerie is saving money for a new backpack. The one she wants costs $57.65. If she saves $7.25 a week, about how many weeks will it take her to have enough money for the backpack?

   Ⓐ 6 weeks   Ⓒ 9 weeks
   Ⓑ 8 weeks   Ⓓ 4 weeks

2. Every afternoon Kelvin unpacks cartons and stocks the shelves in the Good Food Market. On Monday he stocked 30 cans of dog food, on Tuesday he stocked 25 boxes of cereal, on Wednesday he stocked 40 cans of tuna fish, on Thursday he stocked 35 boxes of cookies, and on Friday he stocked 55 bags of nuts. What is the average number of food items that Kelvin unpacked and shelved in 1 day?

   Ⓐ 45   Ⓒ 37
   Ⓑ 49   Ⓓ 39

3. The faces of 4 U.S. Presidents are carved into Mount Rushmore in South Dakota. The monument was started in 1927 and was completed in 1941. How long did it take to complete the monument?

   Ⓐ 68 years   Ⓒ 18 years
   Ⓑ 14 years   Ⓓ 24 years

4. Shawn bought film for his camera. He got a roll of film that takes 24 pictures. He took 6 pictures of his dog and 9 pictures of his friends. How many more pictures will he be able to take on this roll?

   Ⓐ 10 pictures   Ⓒ 9 pictures
   Ⓑ 15 pictures   Ⓓ 11 pictures

5. At the basketball game, Jeremy scored 8 baskets (2 points each), Tommy scored 5 baskets and 5 free throws (1 point each), and Joe scored 7 baskets and 3 free throws. How many more points did Joe score then Jeremy?

   Ⓐ 16 points   Ⓒ 17 points
   Ⓑ 2 points   Ⓓ 1 point

6. Yvonne planted 5 times as many tulip bulbs as she planted daffodil bulbs. Altogether she planted 18 bulbs. How many daffodil bulbs did she plant?

   Ⓐ 3 daffodil bulbs   Ⓒ 13 daffodil bulbs
   Ⓑ 223 daffodil bulbs   Ⓓ 8 daffodil bulbs

7. The Alonzo family is planning to go on a 4-day ski trip. They are on a budget and do not want to spend a lot of money for a hotel room. The rate for a family their size ranges from $94 to $158 per day. How much money will they save if they choose the room with the lowest rate rather than the highest rate?

   Ⓐ $94   Ⓒ $64
   Ⓑ $256   Ⓓ $138

8. The Gidden family is planning a 2,000-mile auto trip next summer. On the first day they will stay with friends who live 398 miles away. How many more miles will they have to go to complete their trip?

   Ⓐ 2,398   Ⓒ 1,602
   Ⓑ 2,000   Ⓓ 402

Problem Solving: Measurement, Geometry, and Patterns

Directions Darken the circle for the correct answer.

1. One of the trees in the Cranes' backyard adds $\frac{1}{2}$ foot to its circumference each year. It is about 3 feet around now. Ray and his friends decided to guess what the tree's circumference would be in 10 years. Giselle thought the circumference would be 8 feet, Carlos thought it would be 5 feet, Benji thought it would be 13 feet, and Ray thought is would be 6 feet. Who is right?

Ⓐ Ray   Ⓒ Carlos
Ⓑ Giselle   Ⓓ Benji

2. Donna takes care of two cats five days a week. Before she leaves for school each morning, she gives them food and water. This takes her about 15 minutes. In the afternoon she plays with the cats for 30 minutes. How many minutes a week does Donna take care of the cats?

Ⓐ 375 minutes   Ⓒ 45 minutes
Ⓑ 225 minutes   Ⓓ 60 minutes

3. Sandy is making clothespin dolls to sell at a craft show. She makes 1 doll the first day, 5 the second day, 9 the third day, and so on. How many dolls will Sandy have altogether after 5 days?

Ⓐ 13 dolls   Ⓒ 45 dolls
Ⓑ 17 dolls   Ⓓ 159 dolls

4. Vivian is training to enter a walk-a-thon. She walked 6 miles the first week, 9 miles the second week, 12 miles the third week, and 15 miles the fourth week. If this pattern continues, how many miles will she walk the next week?

Ⓐ 18 miles   Ⓒ 19 miles
Ⓑ 16 miles   Ⓓ 17 miles

5. Lucinda is baking cookies. She is making two kinds of dough, chocolate and vanilla. She will use nuts, raisins, and chocolate chips to decorate the cookies. She will use only one kind of decoration on each cookie. How many different kinds of cookies will she be able to make?

Ⓐ 3   Ⓒ 6
Ⓑ 5   Ⓓ 2

6. Dr. Trecino holds office hours on Monday, Tuesday, and Thursday from 9:15 A.M. to 11:45 A.M. and again from 2:15 P.M. to 6:30 P.M. How many hours does she spend in her office altogether on those days?

Ⓐ 6 hours and 45 minutes
Ⓑ 5 hours and 30 minutes
Ⓒ 18 hours and 30 minutes
Ⓓ 20 hours and 15 minutes

7. The Adams family is building an enclosed run for their dog. The run will be 75 yards long and 15 yards wide. What will the total number of feet in the perimeter of the run be?

Ⓐ 180 feet   Ⓒ 540 feet
Ⓑ 1,125 feet   Ⓓ 270 feet

Problem Solving: Fractions, Decimals, and Percent

Directions Darken the circle for the correct answer.

1. The faces of the Presidents are each 60 feet high. The nose on each face is 20 feet long. Which fraction shows what part of the height of the face is the length of the nose?

   Ⓐ $\frac{1}{3}$ Ⓒ $2\frac{1}{3}$

   Ⓑ $\frac{2}{3}$ Ⓓ $1\frac{2}{3}$

2. Luis works in a pizza parlor. He works $7\frac{1}{2}$ hours each day. He spends $\frac{5}{6}$ of the time making pizzas. For the rest of the time, he waits on customers. How many hours a day does Luis spend making pizzas?

   Ⓐ 6 hours   Ⓒ $6\frac{1}{4}$ hours

   Ⓑ $5\frac{1}{2}$ hours   Ⓓ 7 hours

3. A recent newspaper article about the activities of retired people showed that $\frac{1}{3}$ of them enjoyed golfing and swimming, and $\frac{1}{12}$ of them enjoyed doing arts and crafts. What fraction of the total group does other things?

   Ⓐ $\frac{7}{12}$ Ⓒ $\frac{5}{12}$

   Ⓑ $\frac{1}{2}$ Ⓓ $\frac{2}{3}$

4. Mr. Schroeder's rose farm had 620 rosebushes. He sold 50% of the bushes. How many bushes did he sell?

   Ⓐ 325   Ⓒ 350

   Ⓑ 310   Ⓓ 315

5. The average yearly snowfall in Concordia is 22.9 centimeters. Last winter they had 26.3 centimeters of snow. How much more snow than usual did Concordia have last winter?

   Ⓐ 6.6 centimeters
   Ⓑ 2.3 centimeters
   Ⓒ 4.5 centimeters
   Ⓓ 3.4 centimeters

6. Sofia is on the basketball team in her school. She stays after school for 1 hour on Tuesday and Wednesday, and $\frac{1}{2}$ hour on Thursday to practice shooting baskets. If she takes about 32 shots per hour, how many times does she shoot for the basket in 1 week?

   Ⓐ 75 times   Ⓒ 80 times

   Ⓑ 60 times   Ⓓ 50 times

7. The average TV set uses 0.225 kilowatt-hours (kwh). If it costs $.09 per hour to run the TV, how much would it cost to keep the TV on from 11:30 A.M. to 4:30 P.M. for 5 days?

   Ⓐ $4.50   Ⓒ $2.25

   Ⓑ $5.00   Ⓓ $7.25

8. The football team won 7 out of 10 games. What percent did the team win?

   Ⓐ 7%   Ⓒ 70%

   Ⓑ 30%   Ⓓ 50%

Problem Solving: Estimation and Pre-Algebra

Directions Darken the circle for the correct answer.

1. Carmelo's Restaurant bought 32 boxes of napkins. There were 250 napkins in each box. What is the best estimate of the number of napkins the restaurant bought?

  Ⓐ 5,000   Ⓒ 12,000
  Ⓑ 7,500   Ⓓ 90,000

2. Mr. Wilson raises about 12 goats per acre of pasture. His ranch has 956 acres of pastureland. About how many goats does he raise altogether?

  Ⓐ 1,000   Ⓒ 7,000
  Ⓑ 1,300   Ⓓ 12,000

3. Two books cost $5.98 together. One of the books cost $1.89. What is the closest estimate of the cost of the other book?

  Ⓐ $3   Ⓒ $4
  Ⓑ $2   Ⓓ $1.50

4. The Bennett family invited 15 guests for Thanksgiving dinner. The turkey cost $16.50, and the pumpkin pies cost $14.20. About how much will they spend on each guest for turkey and pumpkin pie?

  Ⓐ $30.60   Ⓒ $2.00
  Ⓑ $19.20   Ⓓ $31.60

5. Maida sells hand-knit hats for $46.95 each. Last week she sold 8 hats. What is the best estimate of how much money she earned for the hats?

  Ⓐ $100   Ⓒ $300
  Ⓑ $200   Ⓓ $400

6. Last week Faren and his brother Bert went downtown by bus. At the first stop the bus made, 3 people got off and 2 got on. At the second stop, 5 people got off and 4 got on. At the third stop, 2 people got off and 3 got on. There were 15 people left on the bus when Faren and Bert came to their stop. How many people were on the bus before the first stop?

  Ⓐ 16 people   Ⓒ 13 people
  Ⓑ 18 people   Ⓓ 17 people

7. Mr. Ramirez raises Christmas trees on his farm. The smallest tree that he sells measures $1\frac{1}{2}$ meters. Each row of trees on his farm has 64 trees. The last time he checked his records, he had 2 rows of trees that measured 3 meters, 4 rows that measured 6 meters, 8 rows that measured 5 meters, and 10 rows that measured $1\frac{1}{2}$ meters. He has an order for 320 trees that must be either 5 or 6 meters tall. If he ships 4 rows of 5-meter trees, how many rows of 6-meter trees will he have to ship?

  Ⓐ 3 rows   Ⓒ 6 rows
  Ⓑ 5 rows   Ⓓ 1 row

8. Theresa's class is going on an outing. Eight students want to go hiking. Ten students want to go swimming. Three students would like to do both activities. How many students want to do at least one of the activities?

  Ⓐ eight students   Ⓒ fifteen students
  Ⓑ ten students   Ⓓ three students

Name _____ Date _____

Science Overall Assessment

Directions Darken the circle for the correct answer.

1. Geothermal power is produced ____.

Ⓐ by the Sun   Ⓑ by the wind   Ⓒ inside the Earth   Ⓓ through lightning

2. A trait that is stronger than another trait is called ____.

Ⓐ dominant   Ⓑ recessive   Ⓒ inherited   Ⓓ fossilized

3. When a sperm cell joins an egg cell, the egg cell is ____.

Ⓐ fertilized   Ⓑ destroyed   Ⓒ fossilized   Ⓓ dominant

4. The way an organism looks and acts can be affected by ____ and environment.

Ⓐ weather   Ⓑ heredity   Ⓒ wishing   Ⓓ biome

5. ____ is a mixture in which one of the parts is a liquid.

Ⓐ A suspension   Ⓑ A solution   Ⓒ A mixture   Ⓓ A colloid

6. A hurricane may develop in ____.

Ⓐ a cold polar ocean   Ⓑ a warm tropical ocean   Ⓒ any ocean   Ⓓ a river

7. Inherited behavior traits that help animals to stay alive are called ____.

Ⓐ instructions   Ⓑ instincts   Ⓒ internal   Ⓓ recessive

8. The average weather of a place over time is its ____.

Ⓐ biome   Ⓑ global warming   Ⓒ climate   Ⓓ temperature

9. The climate of areas near the equator is ____.

Ⓐ temperature   Ⓑ polar   Ⓒ microclimate   Ⓓ tropical

10. Igneous rocks are formed when ____.

Ⓐ gravity causes particles to become layered
Ⓑ hot, melted rock cools and hardens
Ⓒ rocks break into tiny pieces
Ⓓ rivers deposit materials along the banks

Earth and Space Science

Directions Darken the circle for the correct answer.

1. To support life the biosphere needs ____.

Ⓐ sunlight, air, water, and minerals
Ⓑ solids, liquids, and gases
Ⓒ clouds, rain, and wind
Ⓓ topsoil, subsoil, and bedrock

2. The process of rocks breaking down into small pieces is ____.

Ⓐ weathering
Ⓑ strip mining
Ⓒ refining
Ⓓ insulating

3. Remains of past life that are found in rocks are ____.

Ⓐ molds
Ⓑ fossils
Ⓒ casts
Ⓓ drifts

4. Water covers ____ of the Earth's surface.

Ⓐ 20%
Ⓑ 30%
Ⓒ 50%
Ⓓ 70%

5. A twisting, funnel-shaped storm is a ____.

Ⓐ squall line
Ⓑ hurricane
Ⓒ blizzard
Ⓓ tornado

6. The smallest building block of matter is the ____.

Ⓐ molecule
Ⓑ element
Ⓒ atom
Ⓓ compound

7. Plants give off ____ as a waste product.

Ⓐ carbon dioxide
Ⓑ oxygen
Ⓒ nitrogen
Ⓓ sugar

8. The Moon's gravitational pull on the Earth and on bodies of water on it causes ____.

Ⓐ tides
Ⓑ precipitation
Ⓒ pollution
Ⓓ earthquakes

9. Food wastes, leaves, grass, and wood are ____.

Ⓐ biomes
Ⓑ minerals
Ⓒ climate
Ⓓ organic waste

10. Which of these is a fossil fuel?

Ⓐ natural gas
Ⓑ wood
Ⓒ water
Ⓓ iron

11. The low areas between mountains are called ____.

Ⓐ plateaus
Ⓑ valleys
Ⓒ plains
Ⓓ glaciers

12. What is the shape of the Milky Way?

Ⓐ round
Ⓑ rectangular
Ⓒ spiral
Ⓓ square

Earth and Space Science, p. 2

Directions Answer each question in complete sentences.

1. What are the three steps in the water cycle?

_____

_____

_____

2. What is a molecule?

_____

_____

_____

3. Why can water break rocks when it freezes?

_____

_____

_____

4. What does the word *geothermal* mean?

_____

_____

_____

5. What characteristics do all air masses have in common?

_____

_____

_____

_____

Life Science

Directions Darken the circle for the correct answer.

1. The beat of your heart felt through the skin is ____.

   Ⓐ an energy   Ⓑ a calorie   Ⓒ a pulse   Ⓓ respiration

2. ____ moves blood through the body.

   Ⓐ Respiration   Ⓑ Circulation   Ⓒ Digestion   Ⓓ Excretion

3. A process in which green plants use light energy to make food is called ____.

   Ⓐ photosynthesis   Ⓑ calories   Ⓒ hydration   Ⓓ ecology

4. The study of the relationship between living things and their environment is ____.

   Ⓐ photosynthesis   Ⓑ respiration   Ⓒ ecology   Ⓓ geology

5. Animals that eat only plants are called ____.

   Ⓐ herbivores   Ⓑ omnivores   Ⓒ nucleus   Ⓓ scavengers

6. The division of a cell begins in its ____.

   Ⓐ center   Ⓑ nucleus   Ⓒ cytoplasm   Ⓓ wall

7. ____ reproduction is reproduction by only one parent.

   Ⓐ Sexual   Ⓑ Hereditary   Ⓒ Asexual   Ⓓ Binary

8. Chromosomes carry ____ that determine an organism's traits.

   Ⓐ jeans   Ⓑ genes   Ⓒ organelles   Ⓓ colors

9. When an organism forms a new organism from only a part of the original, it is called ____.

   Ⓐ generation   Ⓑ relocation   Ⓒ regeneration   Ⓓ energy

10. A ____ is a reaction behavior that is done without thought.

   Ⓐ reflex   Ⓑ relax   Ⓒ relay   Ⓓ resorb

Life Science, p. 2

Directions Answer each question in complete sentences.

1. Why is the waste gas that green plants give off during photosynthesis important to us?

   _____

   _____

   _____

2. What can you do to help endangered species?

   _____

   _____

3. Name a food source for each nutrient listed.

   A. carbohydrate   _____

   B. fat   _____

   C. protein   _____

   D. vitamin   _____

4. Why can drinking alcohol be dangerous?

   _____

   _____

   _____

5. Name two ways people can reduce stress or cope with stressful situations.

   _____

   _____

   _____

   _____

Physical Science

Directions Darken the circle for the correct answer.

1. A ramp is a simple machine called _____.

   Ⓐ a fulcrum   Ⓑ an inclined plane   Ⓒ a lever   Ⓓ a pulley

2. Work is measured in _____.

   Ⓐ protons   Ⓑ seconds   Ⓒ meters   Ⓓ joules

3. The force needed to lift an object is equal to its _____.

   Ⓐ size   Ⓑ height   Ⓒ weight   Ⓓ speed

4. A crowbar is a kind of _____.

   Ⓐ fulcrum   Ⓑ inclined plane   Ⓒ lever   Ⓓ pulley

5. A solution is always a _____.

   Ⓐ mixture   Ⓑ liquid   Ⓒ compound   Ⓓ gas

6. Matter that does not have a definite size or shape is a _____.

   Ⓐ solid   Ⓑ gas   Ⓒ liquid   Ⓓ rock

7. Solids tend to hold their shape because _____.

   Ⓐ the molecules are widely spaced
   Ⓑ there is a great pull between the molecules
   Ⓒ solids have few molecules
   Ⓓ the molecules are moving very fast

8. Appliances with higher wattage ratings _____.

   Ⓐ cost more to run
   Ⓑ need fuses
   Ⓒ are less expensive to run
   Ⓓ do not need fuses

9. Electricity can be made from _____.

   Ⓐ wind, lightning, and Sun energy
   Ⓑ Sun, water, and lightning energy
   Ⓒ Sun, water, and nuclear energy
   Ⓓ wind, Sun, and green plant energy

Physical Science, p. 2

Directions Answer the questions in complete sentences.

1. What are the three forms of matter?

_____

_____

2. Name three properties, or characteristics, of matter.

_____

_____

_____

3. Name three simple machines.

_____

_____

_____

4. Name three sources of energy in addition to fuels.

_____

_____

_____

5. What do we call energy from the Sun?

_____

6. What is another name for petroleum?

_____

Name _____ Date _____

Science Portfolio Assessment

Student's Name _____

Date _____

Goals	Evidence and Comments
1. Growth in understanding science concepts	
2. Growth in using science processes	
3. Growth in thinking critically	
4. Growth in developing positive habits of mind and positive attitudes toward science	

Social Studies Overall Assessment

Directions Darken the circle for the correct answer.

1. The movement of people from place to place in a seasonal pattern is called ____.

   Ⓐ cultural diffusion   Ⓒ subsistence
   Ⓑ division of labor   Ⓓ migration

2. Which of the following statements best explains why people first moved from Asia to North America?

   Ⓐ The people were escaping a drought in Asia.
   Ⓑ The people were fleeing from wild animals.
   Ⓒ The people were searching for food.
   Ⓓ The people were fleeing from a cruel leader.

3. The first farming settlements were located in ____.

   Ⓐ river valleys   Ⓒ mountains pastures
   Ⓑ tropical rain forests   Ⓓ arid deserts

4. All power and authority in the government of Egypt belonged to the ____.

   Ⓐ middle class   Ⓒ scribes
   Ⓑ priests   Ⓓ pharaoh

5. Charity, kindness, hard work, good faith, and courtesy are the five virtues of ____.

   Ⓐ Daoism   Ⓒ Hinduism
   Ⓑ Confucianism   Ⓓ Zoroastrianism

6. In India's caste system, ____.

   Ⓐ everyone takes turns doing the unpleasant work of society
   Ⓑ people are born into a certain status and remain in it their entire lives
   Ⓒ people must take examinations to get government jobs
   Ⓓ people are free to practice the religion of their choice

7. Greek ideas, language, and culture were spread throughout North Africa and Southwest Asia by ____.

   Ⓐ Alexander   Ⓑ Augustus   Ⓒ Julius Caesar   Ⓓ Pericles

8. Men in Sparta spent most of their life preparing to be ____.

   Ⓐ government officials   Ⓒ traders and merchants
   Ⓑ soldiers   Ⓓ priests

9. Government decisions in Athens were made by ____.

   Ⓐ an oligarchy   Ⓒ majority rule
   Ⓑ the ostraca   Ⓓ the ten tribunes

Social Studies Overall Assessment, p. 2

Directions Darken the circle for the correct answer.

1. Japan was organized under a ____.

   Ⓐ caste system   Ⓒ feudal system
   Ⓑ civil scrvice system   Ⓓ pueblo system

2. The Incas held their huge empire together by ____.

   Ⓐ adopting the Justinian Code
   Ⓑ making Islam the official religion
   Ⓒ making all citizens take a civil service test
   Ⓓ building a system of wide stone roads

3. Salt was worth a great deal in West Africa because it was used ____.

   Ⓐ to warm the floors of homes   Ⓒ in religious services
   Ⓑ to dry out wood for building   Ⓓ to keep meat from rotting

4. Fear of the unknown was a great barrier to travel across the ____.

   Ⓐ Silk Road   Ⓒ Pacific Ocean
   Ⓑ Indian Ocean   Ⓓ Sahara

5. Many ideas of the Renaissance came from ____.

   Ⓐ Italian navigators and sailors   Ⓒ the Catholic Church
   Ⓑ the teachings of Martin Luther   Ⓓ Greek and Roman learning

6. The completion of the Suez Canal ____.

   Ⓐ gave the United States control over Egypt
   Ⓑ resulted in the Boxer Rebellion
   Ⓒ shortened the sea route from Europe to Asia
   Ⓓ made it easier to travel between North America and South America

7. What was the policy of the United States toward World War I when the war began?

   Ⓐ The United States joined the Triple Alliance.
   Ⓑ The United States joined the Triple Entente.
   Ⓒ The United States supported the actions of Germany.
   Ⓓ The United States tried to remain neutral.

8. The purpose of the U.S. policy of détente toward communist nations was to ____.

   Ⓐ force the Soviets to remove their missiles from Cuba
   Ⓑ relax tensions between the Soviet Union and the United States
   Ⓒ end the fighting in Afghanistan
   Ⓓ end the fighting in Vietnam

Name _____ Date _____

Social Studies Overall Assessment, p. 3

Directions Answer each question with complete sentences.

1. What is the difference between a cash-crop economy and a subsistence-farming economy?

_____

_____

_____

_____

2. What were some of the accomplishments of Alexander the Great?

_____

_____

_____

_____

3. How did the Aztecs and Incas make changes in their environments?

_____

_____

_____

_____

4. Why was Ferdinand Magellan's sea journey important? Give three reasons.

_____

_____

_____

_____

5. Why did Britain become the first industrialized country? Give three reasons.

_____

_____

_____

_____

Reading Maps

Directions Use the information in the political map and the cartogram showing population size in countries of South America. Answer the following questions.

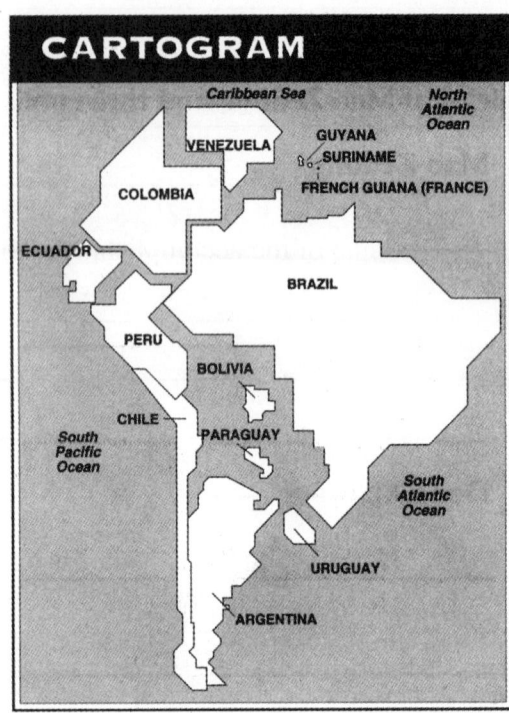

1. Compare Ecuador and Paraguay. Which country has the larger area? Which country has the greater population? _____

   _____

2. Compare Argentina and Peru. Which country has the larger area? Which country has the greater population? _____

   _____

3. Which country has the largest area and the greatest population? _____

4. Which country has the smallest area and the smallest population? _____

5. What ocean is located west of South America? _____

Name _____ Date _____

Reading Graphs

Directions Trade between Britain and the American colonies was an important economic activity in the early eighteenth century. Use the information in this graph to answer the following questions.

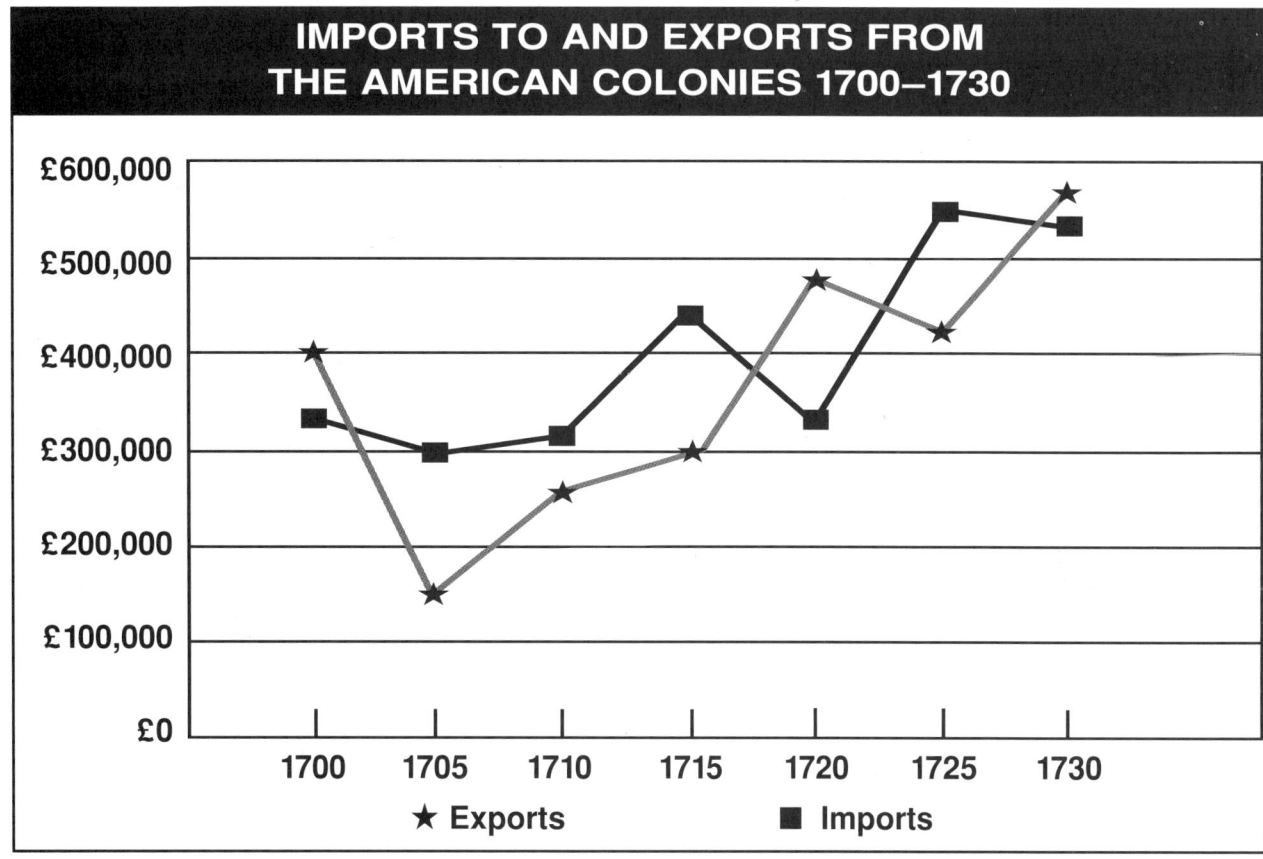

IMPORTS TO AND EXPORTS FROM THE AMERICAN COLONIES 1700–1730

★ Exports   ■ Imports

1. In which years were exports greater than imports? _____

2. When were exports from the colonies the greatest? _____

3. When were imports into the colonies the fewest? _____

4. Which was greater in 1710—exports or imports? _____

5. Which was greater in 1700—exports or imports? _____

Name _____ Date _____

Reading Time Lines

(Directions) Use the information in the time lines to answer the questions.

Telescoped Time Line

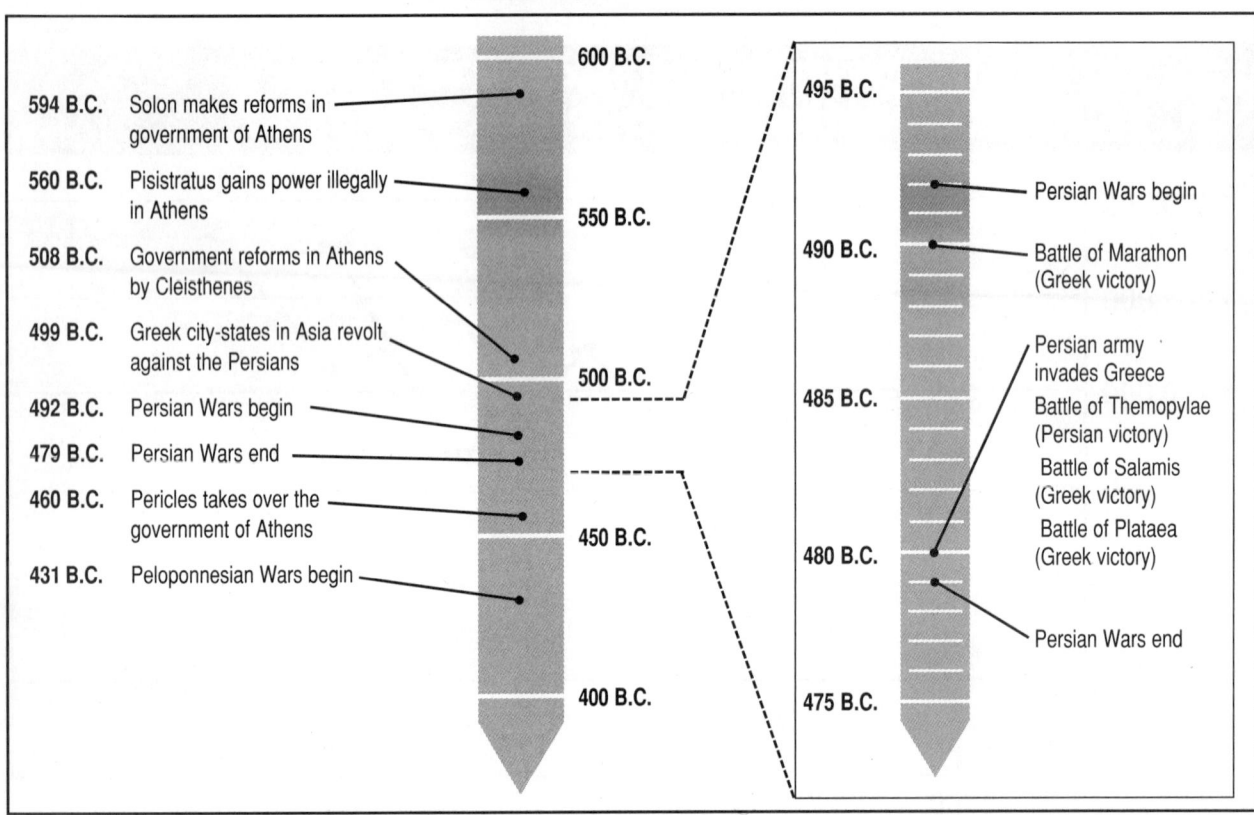

1. Why is there a telescoped time line for this period?

_____

_____

2. What year did the Persian Wars begin?

_____

3. Which event took place first, the Battle of Salamis or the reforms of Cleisthenes?

_____

4. Which event took place last, the Battle of Marathon or the Battle of Themopylae?

_____

5. During what year did Solon make reforms in the government of Athens?

_____

Skills Assessments, Grade 6
Answer Key

Page 5
1. B
2. D
3. B
4. B
5. C
6. A
7. A
8. C
9. Fact
10. Inference

Page 6
1. B
2. A
3. D
4. C
5. The children could learn how to save money by turning off radios and stereos. OR The children could learn how to save energy.

Page 7
1. A
2. A
3. C
4. B
5. C
6. B
7. C
8. A
9. B
10. A

Page 8
1. C
2. D
3. B
4. C
5. B
6. D
7. B
8. D
9. B
10. C

Page 9
1. B
2. D
3. B
4. C
5. D
6. C
7. C
8. B
9. B
10. C

Page 10
1. C
2. A
3. A
4. C
5. B
6. B
7. A
8. C
9. C
10. D

Page 11
1. D
2. D
3. A
4. C
5. B
6. D
7. C
8. A
9. C
10. C

Page 12
1. C
2. B
3. B
4. C
5. D
6. A
7. C
8. D
9. B
10. C

Page 13
1. A
2. B
3. B
4. B
5. A
6. A
7. C
8. C
9. B
10. D

Page 14
1. A
2. C
3. B
4. C
5. B
6. A
7. C
8. C
9. A
10. B

Page 15
1. B
2. A
3. D
4. A
5. D
6. C
7. B
8. C
9. B
10. A

Page 16
1. D
2. C
3. C
4. A
5. B

Page 18
1. C
2. B
3. B
4. C
5. 3; 1; 2

Page 19
1. A
2. C
3. B
4. A
5. B

Page 20
1. A
2. A
3. C
4. B

Page 21
1. C
2. D
3. B

Page 22
1. A. Fact
   B. Fact
   C. Inference
   D. Inference
3. A. Inference
   B. Fact
   C. Fact
   D. Inference
2. A. Fact
   B. Inference
   C. Inference
   D. Inference

Page 24
1. C
2. B
3. A
4. D
5. A

Page 26
1. The author's purpose is to warn against quick judgments of other people.
2. The author says it is important to consider all factors that affect a person's decision.
3. Answers will vary. Possible answers: "Don't judge a person until you've walked a mile in his shoes.", "Don't judge a book by its cover.", "Never say never."
4. Answers will vary. Possible answers: Factors to consider are financial pressure, social pressure, stress, home pressures, work pressures, or the weather.
5. The word *financial* refers to money.

Page 28
1. C
2. D
3. C
4. D
5. A

Page 31
1. Althea grew up in Harlem in New York City.
2. Althea played stickball, basketball, and paddle tennis as a child.
3. Two African-American doctors named Dr. Johnson and Dr. Eaton came up with the plan to help Althea.
4. Althea was the first African-American to play at Forest Hills.
5. Althea won the 1957 Wimbledon championship.

Page 34
1. B
2. C
3. A
4. A
5. C
6. A
7. B

Page 37
1. Armstrong and Aldrin took the *Eagle* to the Moon.
2. Astronauts used the radio to talk to Earth.
3. Michael Collins was left in charge of *Apollo 11.*
4. Armstrong's words were, "That's one small step for a man, one giant leap for mankind."
5. Men from *Apollo 11* walked on the Moon on July 20, 1969.
6. The astronauts' footprints will stay on the Moon's surface for years.

Page 38
1. D
2. C
3. B
4. B
5. A
6. B
7. D
8. C
9. A

Page 39
1. B
2. A
3. A
4. A
5. C
6. C
7. The Art of the Plains Indians
8. 709.011
9. title card
10. fiction
11. biography
12. reference
13. periodical
14. nonfiction

Page 40
1. A
2. D
3. C
4. B
5. C
6. C
7. C
8. B
9. C
10. D

Page 41
1. D
2. A
3. C
4. A
5. D
6. B
7. C
8. C
9. C
10. A

Page 42
1. D
2. B
3. C
4. C
5. D
6. The, My
7. Have
8. Stand, Me
9. The
10. The, Children's, Hour

Page 43
1. B
2. C
3. A
4. B
5. C
6. B
7. A
8. C
9. C
10. A

Page 44
1. B
2. A
3. C
4. B
5. B
6. B
13. river
14. planet
15. girl or name
16. country
17. desert
18. city or capital
7.–12. Answers will vary

Page 45
1. C
2. B
3. A
4. C
5. C
6. A
7. A
8. B
9. C
10. C
11. C
12. B
13. A
14. A
15. B
16. C
17. B
18. A
19. C
20. A

Page 46
1. A
2. B
3. C
4. A
5. A
6. C
7. B
8. C
9. C
10. B
11. A
12. B
13. C
14. C
15. C
16. B

Page 47
1. B
2. C
3. C
4. D
5. D
6. D
7. A
8. A
9. B
10. C
11. B
12. B

Page 48
1. C
2. A
3. C
4. B
5. D
6. C
7. B
8. C

Page 49
1. IM
2. D
3. IN
4. E
5. RO
6. I
7. CS
8. C
9. A
10. D
11. B
12. C
13. A
14. C
15. D

Page 50
1. D
2. C
3. B
4. B
5. C
6. A
7. D
8. B
9. A
10. C
11. C
12. C

Page 51
1. B
2. A
3. C
4. C
5. A
6. B
7. D
8. A
9. A
10. C
11. D
12. A

Page 53
1. A
2. D
3. B
4. A
5. B
6. D
7. B
8. D

Page 54
1. C
2. C
3. B
4. A
5. B
6. 3
7. noun
8. p. 135–139

Page 55
1. A
2. B
3. B
4. B
5. A
6. A
7. B
8. C
9. muddy
10. pile

Page 56
1. B
2. D
3. C
4. D
5. A
6. C

Page 57
1. At the beginning of the narrative, the author felt excited, but the author was not expecting to be surprised.
2. At the end, the writer became surprised.
3. The narrative is told in first person.
4. The clue words for first person are my, I, and me.

Page 58
1. 6
2. Pour the orange juice into the bowl.
3. You must not let your friend see you make the punch.

Page 59
1. contrast
2. comparison
3. Answers will vary. Possible answers: Lena complains and argues, but she is more honest. Taylor talks behind someone's back.
4. Answers will vary. Possible answers: intelligent, loyal, helpful, good conversationalists, sense of humor.

Answer Key, p. 2

Page 60

1. Mr. Cratchit is a fine man, and I think you should think carefully before letting him go.
2. 3
3. Bob is quick with numbers.

Page 61

1. The room had clearly been ransacked.
2. Answers may vary. A word or phrase that appeals to the sense of smell is "fragrance" or "garlic."
3. Answers may vary. "Crunched loudly underfoot" appealed to the sense of touch.
4. Answers may vary. Space order was indicated by "next to," "trail led," "underfoot," or "on the wall."

Page 62

1. B	6. C	11. A
2. A	7. A	12. C
3. D	8. A	13. D
4. A	9. C	14. C
5. C	10. C	

Page 63

1. B	4. B	7. B
2. A	5. A	8. B
3. A	6. A	

Page 64

1. C	5. C	9. A
2. B	6. B	10. D
3. B	7. D	11. C
4. D	8. A	12. B

Page 65

1. C	5. A	9. B
2. C	6. D	10. C
3. A	7. B	11. A
4. C	8. B	12. C

Page 66

1. C	5. B	9. D
2. C	6. B	10. B
3. B	7. D	
4. B	8. A	

Page 67

1. B	5. C	9. C
2. C	6. A	10. A
3. B	7. D	
4. D	8. B	

Page 68

1. B	4. B	7. C
2. C	5. A	8. A
3. B	6. A	

Page 69

1. D	5. B	9. D
2. B	6. B	10. A
3. C	7. A	
4. B	8. A	

Page 70

1. B	5. C	9. A
2. D	6. A	10. B
3. C	7. C	
4. C	8. A	

Page 71

1. C	5. C	9. A
2. C	6. A	10. D
3. B	7. A	11. A
4. B	8. B	12. A

Page 72

1. B	5. B
2. C	6. A
3. B	7. B
4. C	8. B

Page 73

1. D	5. D	9. C
2. D	6. D	10. C
3. D	7. B	
4. C	8. C	

Page 74

1. 2, 3.5, 5, 6.5, 8	6. 2	
2. a, b, e	7. 12	
3. b, c	8. third	
4. second	9. 5	
5. fifth		

Page 75

1. C	5. D	9. C
2. B	6. C	10. A
3. B	7. B	
4. B	8. B	

Page 76

1. A	5. B	9. D
2. A	6. D	10. B
3. C	7. C	
4. B	8. B	

Page 77

1. B	4. C	7. B
2. C	5. D	8. C
3. B	6. A	

Page 78

1. B	4. A	7. C
2. B	5. C	
3. C	6. D	

Page 79

1. A	5. D
2. C	6. C
3. A	7. C
4. B	8. C

Page 80

1. B	5. D
2. D	6. A
3. C	7. D
4. C	8. C

Page 81

1. C	5. A	9. D
2. A	6. B	10. B
3. A	7. B	
4. B	8. C	

Page 82

1. A	5. D	9. D
2. A	6. C	10. A
3. B	7. B	11. B
4. D	8. A	12. C

Page 83

1. The three steps in the water cycle are evaporation, condensation, and precipitation.
2. A molecule is the combination of two or more atoms.
3. Water can break rocks when it freezes because it expands.
4. *Geothermal* means Earth heat.
5. An air mass has about the same temperature, pressure, and humidity throughout.

Page 84

1. C	5. A	9. C
2. B	6. B	10. A
3. A	7. C	
4. C	8. B	

Page 85

1. Oxygen is the waste gas, and people and animals need it to breathe.

Page 85 cont....

2. Answers will vary. Possible answers: You can avoid products made from endangered species, write to legislators and urge legislation, and educate the world community.
3. Answers will vary. Possible answers: A. carbohydrates: bread, spaghetti, rice, honey, candy, pastry; B. fats: butter, oil, nuts; C. protein: meat, fish, eggs, cheese, milk, peas, nuts, beans; D. vitamins: vegetables, milk, eggs, citrus, fruits, whole-grain cereals.
4. Answers will vary. Possible answers: Drinking alcohol impairs a person's judgment. Alcohol can damage internal organs. Alcohol is dangerous to a pregnant woman's baby and can cause birth defects.
5. Answers will vary. Possible answers: To cope with stress, a person can exercise, participate in a hobby or relaxing activity, call on close friends or family members, get plenty of sleep, eat healthy foods, or get help from a counselor.

Page 86

1. B	4. C	7. B
2. D	5. A	8. A
3. C	6. B	9. C

Page 87

1. The three forms of matter are solids, liquids, and gases.
2. Answers may vary. Possible answers: Properties of matter are color, odor, taste, melting and freezing points, the ability to conduct electricity, and the ability to combine with other materials.
3. Answers may vary. Simple machines are levers, pulleys, inclined planes, wedges, screws, and wheel and axles.
4. Answers may vary. Other sources of energy include water, the Sun, wind, and nuclear energy.
5. Energy from the Sun is called solar energy.
6. Another name for petroleum is oil or crude oil.

Page 89

1. D	4. D	7. A
2. C	5. B	8. B
3. A	6. B	9. C

Page 90

1. C	5. D
2. D	6. C
3. D	7. D
4. C	8. B

Page 91

1. Answers will vary. Possible responses: In a cash-crop economy, crops are sold for cash. [In Colombia, the economy is based on producing a single crop—coffee.] In a subsistence-farming economy, farmers produce only enough food to feed their families. [This is the case in much of Asia and Latin America.]
2. Answers will vary. Possible responses: Alexander wanted to rule not only Greece but also all of the known world. He almost

Page 91 cont....

succeeded. He created the largest empire known up to that time, an empire that was multicultural. Alexander spread Greek culture to Egypt, other parts of North Africa, Southwest Asia, and India. He also built many cities that became centers of learning.
3. Answers will vary. Possible responses: The Aztecs built their capital on an island. They built their houses on posts pounded into the ground. The Aztecs built bridges between the mainland and the islands, and they built aqueducts to carry water to their capital and to their chinampas for growing food. The Incas built a road system throughout their empire. They built bridges across high mountain gorges and constructed stone buildings. The Incas also built terraced hillsides for farming in the mountains.
4. Answers may vary. Possible responses: The first circumnavigation was important for three reasons. First, it showed that Europeans could reach Asia by sailing west. Second, it demonstrated that all the world's oceans were joined together. Third, it enabled geographers to determine the size of the Earth.
5. Answers will vary. Possible responses: There are three reasons that the Industrial Revolution started in Britain. First, there was a spirit present that encouraged people to invent. Second, the country was rich in natural resources, especially iron and coal. And third, British overseas colonies provided markets where the new industrial products could be sold.

Page 92

1. Paraguay has the larger area. Ecuador has the larger population.
2. Argentina has the larger area and population.
3. Brazil
4. French Guiana
5. Pacific Ocean

Page 93

1. 1700, 1720, 1730
2. 1730
3. 1705
4. imports
5. exports

Page 94

1. A telescoped time line allows a closer look at events during a certain period.
2. 492 B.C.
3. reforms of Cleisthenes
4. Battle of Thermopylae
5. 594 B.C.